Toward Positive
Classroom Discipline

Toward Positive Classroom Discipline

HARVEY F. CLARIZIO
Michigan State University

John Wiley & Sons, Inc., New York • London • Sydney • Toronto

Library of Congress Catalogue Card Number: 74-155116

ISBN 0-471-15849-6 (cloth)
ISBN 0-471-15848-8 (paper)

Printed in the United States of America.

10 9 8 7 6 5 4 3 2 1

Preface

Classroom discipline continues to be one of the most difficult problems confronting teachers. The adequate preparation of teachers in this regard has been impeded by the lack of a science of discipline in any strict sense. Today, however, we are witnessing rapid advances in scientific know-how with respect to classroom discipline. These advances, for the most part, have come from the practical applications of learning theory principles. The purpose of this book is to inform both prospective and experienced teachers about these techniques. It also should prove valuable to those professionals (counselors, psychologists, and social workers) who consult with teachers concerning problem children. The techniques discussed here are offered as a starting point in the development of a how-to-do-it book. Thus they are not presented as the final word on disciplinary strategies but, instead, are given as first approximations that undoubtedly will be improved on in the light of further research and experience. In presenting these strategies, I have cited the personal experiences of teachers who have used them as well as the evidence gathered through research carried out in classrooms and related settings. Although the pragmatic import of these techniques is stressed, attention also is devoted to the rationale that underlies these techniques in an effort to guard against blind or mechanical application. What is needed is an approach that combines scientific principles with a genuine concern for the personal and scholastic well-being of our youth—a humanistic behaviorism. Our goal as educators is not to produce conforming automatons but to help develop self-directed human beings.

No attempt has been made to provide a comprehensive study of all the factors that bear on classroom discipline. There is, for example, no discussion of administrative policies, curriculum, class size, home back-grounds, or organic deficits. Instead, I have focused on the teacher and what he can do to promote effective and growth-inducing disciplinary practices. The basic premise of this book is that student behavior or misbehavior is closely related to teacher behavior. A thorough under-standing of the five techniques examined here will enable the teacher to develop disciplinary skills that will advance the social and academic adjustments of his students.

Many people have contributed to the development of this book. Special credit is given to the graduate students and teachers who provided con-crete illustrations of disciplinary strategies in conjunction with class assignments. I especially thank my dedicated assistant, Myrtle Yoshinaga, for her thoughtful reactions.

Harvey F. Clarizio

East Lansing, Michigan

Contents

Toward Positive
Classroom Discipline

1

A Learning Theory Approach to Classroom Discipline

STATEMENT OF THE PROBLEM

Classroom management has always been one of the foremost problems for teachers. Indeed, the adequate control of a class is a prerequisite to achieving instructional objectives and to safeguarding the psychological and physical well-being of students. Control techniques are also of vital concern to students and parents. The student's attitudes toward school as well as the extent of his learnings are influenced to an appreciable degree by the disciplinary factors used by the teacher (Kaplan, 1970). Parents also express considerable interest about the kinds of disciplinary practices employed in the schools—with some parents advocating the use of more stringent controls and others contending that the schools are already too severe and restrictive in their handling of students.

It is well known that many beginning school teachers, whether female or male, are concerned about matters of classroom discipline. In fact, Morse and Wingo (1969) make the assertion that discipline is the biggest problem of beginning teachers. Moreover, school administrators regard the maintenance of discipline as the greatest problem of inexperienced teachers. This problem is by no means limited to the inexperienced; even seasoned teachers can be pushed to their wit's end in coping with deviant behavior. Many veteran teachers readily admit to feeling a need for more practical information about classroom discipline. Furthermore, they complain about finding themselves caught in a double bind, in that they are

1

told to maintain order and then may be subjected to criticism when they do. It is little wonder that many teachers, particularly beginning teachers and those on the secondary level, leave the field because of an inability to cope with problem students.

Some teachers feel that it is not their responsibility to deal with problem children; they assume a Pontius Pilate approach, washing their hands of disciplinary affairs. Realistically, however, it appears that teachers will have little choice in this matter, at least, for the foreseeable future. Despite a doubling of special class provisions for behaviorally disordered children in the public schools between the period 1948 to 1958, only 2 to 5 percent of youngsters thus identified are placed in special classes. This means that approximately 95 to 98 percent of emotionally handicapped pupils are in the regular classes. Bower (1961) contends that, in the average classroom, there are three youngsters who warrant the label emotionally handicapped. Glidewell and Swallow (1968) in their report prepared for the Joint Commission on the Mental Health of Children report that approximately 30 percent of elementary school pupils present some problems of maladjustment, although most of these problems are not severe enough to require clinical attention. About 10 percent of the elementary school students give evidence of problems that are sufficiently severe to justify clinical attention. Thus, even though some teachers would prefer not to concern themselves with the management of problem behavior, this is not likely to be their fate. Although it is true that schools refer more youngsters than any other agency to professionally trained workers, it is equally evident that the teacher, nonetheless, remains the person who has the primary responsibility for the classroom management of the disturbed child. One hour of therapy a week often does little to lessen the need for coping with the child's disturbing behavior during the remaining 35 hours a week that he is in school.

Instead of a decrease in the role of the teacher as it relates to the mental health of children, there is a definite movement in the direction of greater teacher involvement in these matters. Expansion of the teacher's role relative to the student's adjustment has stemmed mainly from the following factors.

1. The shortage of mental health workers has served to force expansion of mental health forces to include school personnel even though their role in this respect has not been clearly conceptualized. Authorities like Redl (1966) point to a need for additional mental health professionals to supplement the traditional clinical team. Some speak of the need for "invisible" therapists.

2. The inadequacy of the clinic model to deal with the varieties of

disturbed children that our society is producing is another factor. In one large urban area, almost three out of every five patients in child psychiatric clinics did not complete treatment (Frumkin, 1955). The abrupt termination of clinic treatments has been ascribed by some authors (Overall and Aronson, 1963) to a discrepancy between the expectations of lower socioeconomic patients and their middle class therapists. Nationally, the fact that only one in four child psychiatric patients receives direct treatment of some kind also highlights the obsolescence of the psychiatric model (Norman, Rosen, and Bahn, 1962). Although we have traditionally modeled intervention after the clinic concept of treatment, the need for a more reality type mental health approach is becoming increasingly recognized. Just as the mounting dissatisfaction with the clinic concept of treatment has led to the development of community psychiatry, so has it led to a new look in school mental health. The current realization that the child's like conditions, for example, the school, are as important as his feelings must obviously involve teachers to a greater extent than was true in the past.

3. The evaluations of therapy with children also have forced us to try other methods. Even with cases for whom the clinic model is supposedly appropriate, for example, middle class neurotic youngsters, the effectiveness of treatment remains to be demonstrated (Bahn et al., 1962). At present, the evidence suggests that anywhere from two thirds to three fourths of disturbed children improve as much without psychological treatment as with it (Levitt, 1963).

4. The rising popularity of learning theory approaches also has resulted in teachers' playing a more central role in the quest for better mental health children. When psychodynamic or Freudian models were the preferred method, the teacher was accorded, at best, a second-string status on the clinical team. Today it might well be the mental health specialist and not the teacher who assumes a supportive role (Gallagher and Chalfant, 1966).

PSYCHIATRIC VERSUS EDUCATIONAL MODEL

The values advocated by educators and by those favoring a psychiatric model often clash, and the clashing of values has led to a role conflict on the part of teachers. The divergence in values espoused by these two groups has been succinctly stated by White (1965). She writes:

It would be fair to say that the mental health movement has rewarded warmth of feeling; spontaneity; insight; a high interest in others, particularly peers; the ability to communicate, especially one's feelings; warm parents; freedom to exercise judgment; warm teachers; and democratic classrooms. The same movement has been against: Being compulsive; competitive striving; intellectualism; being either thing—or achievement-oriented; being emotionally unresponsive, as well as being angry or passionate; being a loner; not confiding in others; teachers who are curriculum-oriented; the regimentation of school like; group tests; red tape; and vice-principals in charge of discipline. Many of these are precisely the values revered by educators committed to the "cognitive" cause.

Because mental health or psychoeducational specialists (psychologists, psychiatrists, social workers, and counselors) have not fully understood the teacher's role, they have made little available to teachers in the way of specific and concrete practical suggestions pertaining to the management of the child's daily behavior. The sad truth is that the mental health concepts advanced by psychodynamically oriented clinicians have proved of little value to teachers on the front lines. Teachers have asked for practical and concrete suggestions, says Morse (1961), only to be given general platitudes. Teachers, therefore, have been forced to rely on their own common sense and ingenuity. Admonitions to be accepting, non-threatening, and understanding of the child's needs have not helped teachers very much in coping with aberrant behavior.[1] In giving advice to educators, mental health professionals seem to forget about the following aspects of the teacher's role, which make it difficult for a teacher to heed their advice. These aspects are as follows.

1. The teacher is a group worker and, therefore, he cannot usually work with just one child.

2. The teacher's primary goal is not to increase the child's personal insights but to achieve certain academic objectives.

3. The teacher must reflect cultural values and, hence, he cannot be permissively accepting.

4. The teacher deals primarily with conscious or preconscious processes and materials.

5. Finally, the teacher must focus on the reality problems as they exist in the situational present.

Because of these basic differences in outlook, the folklore of mental hygiene concepts disseminated in teacher training courses has most likely

[1] Ausubel (1961) opines that permissiveness was, perhaps, over-emphasized during the period between 1935 to 1955 and that there has been a shift away from permissiveness in recent years.

neither promoted the mental health of children nor that of their teachers. In fact, personal adjustment and academic achievement have been viewed as incompatible objectives. Teachers, being asked to do what they cannot, have consequently been made to feel anxious, inadequate, helpless, and guilty with the result that they are less well prepared to fulfill their mental health roles.

THE RATIONALE AND MERITS OF A LEARNING THEORY APPROACH

Although traditional models of personality development and treatment have not yielded much in the way of value to the classroom teacher, an increasingly popular approach—a learning theory approach—has developed that narrows the gap between theory and classroom disciplinary practices.

This approach is more directly concerned with the control of actual *behavior,* for example, hitting others, than with deep-rooted psychological explanations. Accordingly, greater emphasis is devoted to the teaching or training of specific behaviors, for example, getting history assignments completed, than to the development of a sophisticated insight into the remote causes of the maladaptive behavior.

Because some teachers question or feel uncomfortable about the emphasis on behavior per se, it is appropriate to consider some of the reasons why teachers should focus primarily on maladaptive symptoms or behaviors instead of on the underlying causes of the maladaptive behavior. There are several reasons for this emphasis. (1) Teachers, by virtue of their orientation, are not trained to probe the inner dynamics of behavior. They cannot deal with transference neuroses, cannot interpret free associations, or explore dammed up psychic processes. Indeed, psychoeducational specialists (psychologists, counselors, and school social workers) have large gaps in their knowledge relative to the causes of behavior even after they have made extensive diagnostic work-ups. The search for unobservable causes is further complicated by the fact that behavior is typically multiply caused. Rarely is the etiology singular in nature. Not only are there multiple causes, but the causes interact so that specific delineation of the causative factors becomes even more difficult. In certain cases, any one of the component etiological factors may not be sufficient in and of itself to produce deviant behavior. Yet, taken together, these factors may be capable of producing deviant behavior. The difficulties associated with diagnosis in cases of multiple etiologies are illustrated in a study by Lambert and Grossman (1964) in which two teams of psychologists, neurologists, pediatricians, and educators were to determine independently if the learning and behavior difficulties of a given group of students had an organic basis. The results indicated that there was little agreement between the two teams as to the cause of the difficulty for individual students. (2) Assuming that teachers are able to identify or make inferences as to the underlying causes of deviant behavior, they are rarely in a position wherein they can directly manipulate the causes so as to modify their influences on the child's classroom adjustment. For example, if the problem lies in the parent-child relationships or in a brain lesion, there are seldom few, if any, constructive intervention techniques that a teacher can employ. Yet, the child's troublesome behavior persists and must be handled as hygienically as possible. (3) Even in those select cases in which the causes can be identified and manipulated directly, the maladaptive behaviors may persist. Consider the pupil whose reading disability is caused by a combination of faulty child-rearing practices and poor vision. If and when these etiological factors are identified and cleared up, attention still must be focused on his inadequate reading behavior in order for him to be successful in reality. Until these efforts are undertaken, his academic and personal-social adjustment most likely will continue to suffer. (4) In certain cases the behaviors or symptoms may, in and of themselves, become quite incapacitating and, therefore, warrant attention. This point is most dramatically illustrated in certain cases of reading disability wherein the relationships between educational and emotional maladjustment are closely intertwined. (5) There is no reason to believe that when the teacher assists the child in modifying given behaviors that another undesirable behavior will inevitably take its place. Available evidence indicates that there is little support for this Freudian theory of symptom substitution (Grossberg, 1964). Symptomatic treatment of specific behaviors can permit one to break up the vicious circle of maladaptive behavior in which disabling symptoms either intensify the primary problem or become causes in and of themselves. This latter possibility is illustrated in cases of learning disabilities which, although originally symptomatic of a more basic disturbance, come to produce additional anxiety, discomfort, and failure. By modifying the behavior, however, it is sometimes possible to reverse this downward spiral. As the symptomatic behavior begins to clear up, for example, the reading disability, the child is perceived and treated by others in a more favorable light. The parents view him as more worthwhile, as do his peers. Consequently, the child comes to view himself differently and to set new expectations for his own behavior. It is interesting to note that whereas Freudian theorists have always cautioned about the dangers associated with the treatment of specific behavioral symptoms, they have not addressed themselves to the dangers that might result from not treating behavioral symptoms. (6) Finally, as already implied, it is important to notice that the teacher generally has no recourse other than to deal with behavior directly. However, if he can do this effectively, he will have gone far in meeting his responsibilities to his pupils. He should by no means disparage his accomplishments because he has restricted his assistance to the behavioral level. The science of psychology has not yet advanced to the stage that permits far-reaching personality reorganization.

As will be evident from our discussion of the limitations of each technique, we do not envision the methods emanating from learning theory as a panacea. In fact, applications of the five techniques to be considered —positive reinforcement, extinction, punishment, modeling and desensitization—are best regarded as first approximations that will be revised in the light of further experience and research with them. The crucial validation of these techniques must take place in the confines of the regular classroom. Judging from the evidence to date, however, it appears that these techniques do have definite advantages over traditional methods. Foremost among them are the following.

1. The fruitfulness of these techniques in modifying human behavior has been demonstrated in laboratory settings as well as in natural settings. Grounded in research, these techniques enable us to develop systematically trainable competencies among those who are responsible for the building, modifying, and maintaining of behavior patterns in children.

2. They are consistent with the teacher's role whereby he must reflect cultural expectations to the pupils and must set standards for their academic and social behavior. Traditionally, it has been the teacher's job to change the behavior of those entrusted to him.

3. The learning theory approach offers the teacher a variety of management techniques thereby enabling him to expand his repertoire of control skills and to avoid overreliance on any given disciplinary strategy.

4. A learning theory approach offers specific and practical techniques for use in day-to-day classroom problems. Although teachers already use some or all of these techniques, they frequently do so in an intuitive and/or inconsistent way, thereby reducing the efficacy of these intervention tools. The teacher should, in dealing with severe cases, consult with psychoeducational specialists more deeply versed in these techniques. However, the teacher should also be able to cope with the large majority, say 75 percent, of problem students in his class without referral to psychoeducational specialists once behavior modification principles are applied systematically. Indeed, the specific thesis of this book is that teachers can cope effectively

with maladaptive student behaviors within the reality situation of the classroom. We shall show that what the teacher does bear directly on the amount of misbehavior that occurs. The learning theory approach provides concrete ways in which teacher behavior can reduce the amount of problem behavior posed by the students.

5. These techniques enable the teacher to strive toward more realistic and obtainable goals relative to his pupils' academic and personal adjustment. Troublesome "target" behaviors can be selected and then modified through appropriate intervention techniques. One of the major advantages of these techniques is the easy accessibility to observable behaviors that can be readily identified and treated (Ulrich, Stachnik and Mabry, 1966).

6. One of the most important attributes of these techniques is their communicability, that is, they can be taught to teachers. Although there are few if any teacher training institutions currently offering systematic didactic and practicum training in these techniques, one can envision the time when teachers in training will receive these skills in laboratory courses that will be taken in conjunction with their formal course work. In the meantime, teachers in the field may be able to acquire this training through in-service meetings or through workshops. Theoretically, the school psychologist, clinical psychologist, or school counselor, by virtue of his clinical experience and background in learning theory, might well be in a position to conduct training institutes of this kind.

7. In addition to facilitating the teacher's role, the development of a core of behavioral technicians could go far to alleviate the manpower shortage in the mental health disciplines.

Although teachers have long been aware of most of the principles that follow, they have not always been applied in a consistent and planned fashion. Like most human beings, we are inclined to train in a haphazard way. Thus classroom management is based more on mood than on rational intervention with the result that discipline becomes a hit-and-miss proposition. Disciplinary strategies are learned through trial and error and are applied in a similar fashion. This state of affairs is not surprising, since effective discipline typically demands continual watchfulness, consistency, and persistence. On many occasions this requires more energy than we feel we can spare. The simple truth, of course, is that haphazard management practices, although seemingly more economical and less energy consuming, are actually more costly in the long run.

The philosophy associated with a learning theory approach to classroom discipline is not that there are bad teachers who dislike children but, instead, that there are teachers whose skills in training children need improvement. This approach does not state that the teacher must love and "understand" everyone in his class. Although personal warmth is not excluded in this approach, it does not sanctify the teacher-pupil relationship as some mental health approaches would seemingly expect us to do. The learning theory approach does require, however, a professional attitude and commitment that entail the use of the latest and best scientific information available so that teachers can better fulfil their roles as educators.

THREE PHASES

There are three general phases in the use of these principles. First, we observe to find out what *specific* behaviors we want to focus on. We must decide exactly what we want to accomplish with the troublesome student. A note of caution is in order here, since teachers frequently set broad, general objectives without specifying exact steps (subgoals) that must be completed enroute to the main, global objective. Thus, in setting the global objective of "getting him to behave in class," it is necessary to pinpoint the specific behaviors that are to be modified—to stop wiggling or squirming in his seat, to stop getting out of his seat and wandering around the room, to stop talking out of turn, to stop clowning, to refrain from being quarrelsome, to stop laughing at others' shortcomings, to turn in neat papers, and the like. That is, we must select certain target behaviors for attack. Altogether too frequently, we "bite off more than we can chew," that is, our objectives are too broad and too ambitious. We seek to accomplish too much too fast. With maladjusted students, anything approximating total personality change is rarely accomplished. Instead of attempting a global approach to behavioral change at the outset, we recommend a piecemeal approach. Take small steps at a time and pinpoint the behaviors you want to change. What has worked well in practice is asking yourself what are the two or three most bothersome behaviors and to work toward their modification. This molecular approach might appear to be only a small step in terms of what behavioral changes are needed, but it accomplishes more in the long run than does a global, undifferentiated assault on the problem. Once these undesirable behaviors have been selected, the teacher should not try to sneak up on the problem or to make the student guess as to what behavior is unacceptable. Let the student know exactly what is acceptable and what is not. It is also desirable to identify the frequency of the misbehavior, for example, "Sam, are you aware that you did this twelve times yesterday?" (Hunter, 1967). Knowing the frequency of the deviant behavior enables both the teacher and the student to keep track of progress or the lack of it. In summary the teacher should accomplish the following during the first phase:

a. Select the behavior to be changed in a *specific* and *precise* way, since vague objectives often lead to confusion and inconsistency in disciplinary procedures.

b. State the objective in a way that it refers to *observable* behavior that can be counted. That is, the objective should tell you what to look for (for example, handing in homework assignments).

c. State your *standard* for acceptable behavior (for example, studying quietly for 15 minutes).

d. Specify the *context* under which you want the behavior to occur. In other words, the teacher's objective should tell you and the student when and where the desired behavior is supposed to happen (for example, turning in homework at the start of the period) (Neisworth et al., 1969).

e. Record the rate, frequency, and duration of the behavior.

Once these target behaviors have been chosen, ways must be planned to weaken undesirable behaviors (phase two) and plans must be made to strengthen desirable behavior (phase three). As you will see shortly, we often attempt to weaken deviant behaviors through procedures such as extinction and punishment, and to strengthen socially appropriate behaviors through positive reward and modeling. That is, we try to modify certain behaviors and to find new ones to replace them. A common strategy is to strengthen behaviors, for example, studiousness, which compete with unacceptable behaviors, for example, inattentiveness. Another valuable strategy consists in seeing what usually happens right *before* and right *after* the misbehavior. This type of analysis not only enables the teacher to pinpoint events or students that trigger the maladaptive behavior in question but to identify what keeps the misbehavior alive. The following analysis was conducted on clowning behavior.

Before	Behavior	After
Unstructured assignments given—no specific directions given	Pete begins to clown	Teacher pays attention by scolding—peers laugh

Once the teacher identified what led up to the clowning and the payoff for Pete, he was in a much better position to prevent similar situations from arising. At this point let us consider the learning theory techniques themselves.

Following the lead of Millon (1969), we divide the techniques designed to modify behavior into two categories—behavior formation techniques and behavior elimination techniques—on the basis of the primary objective of intervention. The first set of approaches includes techniques designed not only to eliminate undesirable behavior but also to strengthen existent adaptive responses and to acquire new adaptive ones. The two major techniques that will be discussed in this regard are positive reinforcement and social modeling procedures. The second set of approaches are restricted but particularly well-suited to the task of weakening undesirable behaviors. Foremost among them are extinction, punishment, and desensitization procedures.

SUMMARY

Most teachers feel a need to improve their skills in classroom management. The best evidence available indicates that there will be three students (10 percent) with moderate to severe emotional problems in the average classroom. If we include students with mild maladjustment, the figure jumps to nine students (30 percent) per classroom. And, of course, even students capable of mature self-direction can benefit from sound classrooms management. Because the trend today is for increased concern with the student's adjustment, it is imperative that we assist the teacher in meeting this professional responsibility. The type of psychological "help" previously made available not only failed to take into account various aspects of the teacher's role but had as its objective the achievement of greater self-understanding and emotional ventilation instead of changes in the student's real life behavior in the classroom. A learning theory approach to classroom discipline can promote the student's well-being while being consistent with the fulfillment of the professional expectations made on the teacher. Specific merits of this approach are presented. Basically, the application of learning theory principles, as outlined in this book, entails (1) the explicit specification of undesirable behaviors to be modified; (2) the explicit specification of the conditions that provoke and reinforce unacceptable behavior, and (3) the explicit formulation of strategies to alter deviant ways.

REFERENCES

Ausubel, D. A new look at classroom discipline. *Phi Delta Kappan*, 1961, **43**, 25–30.
Bahn, A., Chandler, C., and Eisenberg, L. Diagnostic characteristics related to services in psychiatric clinics for children. *Milbank Memorial Fund Quart.*, 1962, **40**, 289–318.

Bower, E. *The education of emotionally handicapped children.* Sacramento, California: California State Department of Education, 1961.

Frumkin, R. M. Occupation and major mental disorders. In A. M. Rose (ed.), *Mental health and mental disorder.* New York: Norton, 1955, 136–160.

Gallagher, J. J., and Chalfant, J. C. The training of educational specialists for emotionally disturbed and socially maladjusted children. In W. W. Wattenberg (ed.), Social deviancy among youth. *Yearbook Nat. Soc. Stud. Educ.,* 1966, **65**, Part I, 398–422.

Glidewell, J. C., and Swallow, C. S. *The prevalence of maladjustment in elementary schools.* Chicago: The University of Chicago, 1968.

Grossberg, J. Behavior therapy: a review. *Psychol. Bull.,* 1964, **62**, 73–88.

Hunter, M. *Reinforcement.* El Segundo, California: TIP Publications, 1967.

Kaplan, L. *Mental Health and Education.* New York: Harper Row, 1970.

Lambert, N., and Grossman, H. *Problems in determining the etiology of learning and behavior problems.* Sacramento, California: California State Department of Education, 1964.

Levitt, E. Psychotherapy with children: a further review. *Behavior Research and Therapy,* 1963, **1**, 45–51.

Milton, T. *Modern Psychopathology. A Biosocial Approach to Maladaptive Learning and Functioning.* Philadelphia: W. B. Saunders, 1969.

Morse, W. The mental hygiene dilemma in public education. *Amer. J. Orthopsychiat.,* 1961, **31**, 332–338.

Morse, W. C. and Wingo, G. M. *Psychology and Teaching.* Glenview, Illinois: Scott, Foresman and Company, 1969.

Neisworth, J., Deno, S., and Jenkins, J. *Student Motivation and Classroom Management—a behavioristic approach.* Newark, Delaware: Behavior Technics, Inc., 1969.

Norman, V., Rosen, B., and Bahn, A. Psychiatric clinic out-patients in the United States, 1959. *Mental Hygiene,* 1962, **46**, 321–343.

Overall, B., and Aronson, H. Expectations of psychotherapy in patients of lower socioeconomic class. *Amer. J. Orthopsychiat.,* 1963, 33, 421–430.

Redl, F. *When we deal with children.* New York: The Free Press, 1966.

Ulrich, R., Stachnik, T., and Mabry, J. *Control of Human Behavior.* Glenview, Illinois: Scott, Foresman and Company, 1966.

White, M. Little red schoolhouse and little white clinic. *Teachers College Record,* 1965, **67**, 188–200.

2

The Use of Reward

If a behavior results in what we want, we are inclined to repeat it. Behavior, in other words, is in large measure determined by its consequences. For example, if an acting-out student can attract the attention of others by blurting out answers in class, he will probably not raise his hand and wait his turn. Likewise, if he raises his hand and the teacher does not call on him because he has already taken other students' turns, the acting-out child is not likely to follow the "raise your hand" rule. All behaviors must have a payoff of some kind—the attracting of attention, the gaining of power, the expression of hostility toward those we do not like, being left alone (Dreikurs, 1969)—or we discontinue them. If a troublesome behavior, for example, whining, occurs frequently, one can be certain that it has worked, that is has been positively reinforced, or else the misbehavior would not be worth our time and energy.

The giving of rewards constitutes one of the most valuable tools teachers have at their disposal. Teachers have long recognized the importance of rewards and often use them to change behavior. Thus the teacher who says, "I see that Johnny is ready to begin his math now that recess is over" is rewarding Johnny for his attentiveness and studiousness.

One of the merits of this approach stems from its applicability to all students. It is not just for the antisocial student, the culturally disadvantaged, the brain-injured, the emotionally disturbed, or for the normal child. For every student, regardless of the label we attach to him, needs ample rewards if he is to behave and to achieve in school.

13

Despite the efficacy and apparent simplicity of this technique, we often misuse it. Basically, there are two ways in which we violate this principle—through sins of commission and through sins of omission. The former refers to the rewarding of unwanted behavior, whereas the latter refers to the failure to reward desired behavior. Their consequences are nicely illustrated by the study of Madsen and his associates (1968) on sit-down commands. These investigators dealt with a student behavior that has plagued teachers for years, namely, the students' standing up when they are supposed to be working. First, the investigators observed how frequently the target behavior—standing up inappropriately—occurred during a given time interval so as to have a base line for later comparisons. Two types of teacher behavior were also recorded: (a) the number of times that teachers told students to sit down or that they gave reprimands for stand up behaviors, and (b) the number of times a teacher praised students for sitting down. The teachers then were instructed to give "sit down" commands whenever the child was inappropriately out of his seat. During this phase of the experiment, "sit down" commands tripled. What happened? Did the incidence of standing behavior decrease? No, instead it rose dramatically, presumably, because the "sit down" commands served as a reinforcer for the behavior that the demands were to eliminate. The teachers were then instructed to return to their earlier ways of coping with this type of disruptive behavior. The rate of standing behavior fell to its original level. Another "sit down" phase was instituted, and standing behaviors again increased. In the final phase of the program, teachers were given the following rule:

> "Give *praise* and *attention* to behaviors which facilitate learning. Tell the child what he is being praised for. Try to reinforce behaviors incompatible with those you wish to decrease (praise: sitting in seat and working properly, sitting with feet on floor and facing front, etc.)."

Under this regimen wherein desired behavior is strengthened and undesirable behavior is weakened, stand-up behaviors decreased to the point that there were approximately 100 less instances of it per 20-minute period! In addition to pointing out the misuse and proper use of reward, this study highlights the importance of dealing with *specific* behaviors, the potency of catching children at being good, and the technique of strengthening appropriate behaviors that compete with inappropriate behaviors.

Classroom observations reveal that even experienced teachers "sin" by commission and omission. Reflect for a moment on the following "sins of commission." How many times do you in a typical day reinforce:

the negativistic student by "arguing" with him,
the aggressive student by paying attention to him,
the dependent student by doing things for him, or
the whiny student by eventually giving in to him?

Consider the following "sins of omission." How often do you pay attention to:

the talkative child when he is quiet, the hyperactive child when he is in his seat, or the irresponsible student when he turns in an assignment?

How often do you phone or jot the parent a note when the disorderly child had a good day?

Do you ever send the problem child to the office so that the principal can reinforce the student's acceptable behavior?

How often do you put the child's name on the board when he is good?

It is easy to understand how teachers inadvertently reward undesirable behavior. As many of us know too well, it is natural to pay attention to the problem behavior regardless of how busy we may be. Generally, the teacher gets reinforced for yelling or threatening the acting-out student in that these tactics on the teacher's part lead to short-term changes in the student's behavior. Unfortunately, however, even though the student may desist momentarily, the troublesome behavior may actually accidentally be strengthened in that it effectively elicits teacher attention. Just as teachers train students, students also train teachers. In this case, they train us to shout and to become upset over them. Such attention, although unpleasant, is nonetheless better than none. Since both the teacher and the student are reinforced for their behaviors, they continue using them. Ideally, or ultimately, teachers should pay attention to disorderly students only when they do what teachers want them to do.

We all realize that we should reward desirable behavior, but there are discrepancies between what we know and what we do. The question arises as to why we miss so many opportunities to strengthen the very kind of behaviors that we want to develop in our students. Four explanations come to mind.

One reason is that we develop such negative perceptions of the misbehaving pupil that we do not see what he does right. It is his misbehavior that catches our eye. We do not expect this kind of child to behave and thus we do not see his proper conduct. Perception is a very selective process. On many occasions I have asked teachers what a disorderly student does right. The standard reply is nothing or not much. Yet, when given a description of an average day's events, it is apparent that the student engages in many behaviors that the teacher could commend. But we simply fail to notice him when he quiets down or slows down.

Second, even when we do see him behave, it is very difficult to reward someone who gives us a bad time. We are simply not inclined to do so. It is hard to be nice to people who are not nice to us. This reaction on our part makes it difficult for us to reward such a child. How many times have we, on seeing a disorderly child behaving, said to ourselves something to the effect that, "This won't last long. He'll be back to his old tricks before long." Let's face it—the disorderly pupil makes our job doubly difficult. Our days go well when he is absent, and we give a sigh of relief when he does not put in an appearance in the morning.

Third, the teacher has a natural tendency to "let-down," and catch her breath once the problem child does quiet down. We are quite content to leave him alone once he settles down. Or else we feel, justifiably so, that we must start paying attention to the other 30 students in the class. After all, we are group workers.

Finally, we simply expect all students to behave. After all, we reason, is it not the student's role to meet our expectations? Why should we give the disorderly student extra payoffs when he is only doing what everyone else in the class does without apparent reward. Giving extra privileges, we reason, is unfair to the other students.[1] This type of cultural value relating to a middle class sense of duty and fairness interferes with our becoming effective sources of reward for students. While teachers feel that it is fair to individualize classroom instruction in reading, or math, they feel that it is unjust to individualize their policies regarding classroom discipline. We often are quite willing to gear academic kinds of instruction to the student's intellectual readiness but frequently we are unwilling to adjust discipline practices to the child's level of social and emotional readiness.

It is not surprising that students act up, since too frequently one of the surest ways to lose teacher attention is to do what one is expected to do. We can hardly expect students to comply with classroom ground rules when, for instance, the loss of teacher attention results from the pursuit of desirable classroom performances. The writer recalls consulting with a Head Start teacher who complained that she could not get an "emotionally starved" child in her class to remain seated. When queried as to how much time she spent with the child when she (the student) was seated, it became evident that the teacher would ignore the student

---

[1] Many teachers view rewards as "bribes." The equating of these two terms overlooks an important distinction between them. Bribes are designed to produce morally corrupt behaviors whereas rewards, as referred to here, are used to develop and to strengthen socially appropriate behaviors.

who would work diligently at her desk for as long as 15 minutes at one time. The student's good behavior did not pay off, that is, it did not achieve the results she wanted so desperately, namely, attention from her teacher. Getting out of her seat and spending as much time as she could around the teacher's desk did get her what she wanted, however.

THREE FACTORS IN THE USE OF REWARD

In this section, we discuss three factors that must be given consideration if the successful application of positive reinforcement is to be achieved. Basically, the teacher must answer questions relating to the frequency of reward, the timing of reward, and the type of reward to be used.

How Often Should I Give a Reward?

With respect to the frequency of rewards, a distinction must be made between the acquisition (that is, learning or building) of a behavior and its maintenance. When the teacher wants a student to learn a new behavior, he should ideally reward the student *every time* the given behavior occurs.[2] Thus, for example, the habitually hostile child who makes a friendly, cooperative, or nonaggressive response toward a classmate should be rewarded *every time* he does so. Rewarding him once or twice is not enough. We must do it again and again on a *regular* basis until his cooperative behavior toward others has been securely acquired. At that point it is no longer necessary to give frequent rewards. In fact, it then would be best that the teacher reinforce such behavior every now and then (intermittent reinforcement) rather than 100 percent of the time, since this schedule of reinforcement renders the behavior less subject to forgetting. Similarly, the basically shy child should be reinforced for greater assertiveness 100 percent of the time until assertiveness becomes a fairly established response for him. Once this point has been reached, you need no longer be concerned with the learning of this more desirable mode of behaving, since this has been accomplished. Now the problem centers around the maintenance of behavior, that is, with how long he will remember to behave this way once you are occupied with other students or activities and cannot reward him regularly. After all, to get along in the classroom, he has to behave appropriately without

[2] In actual practice, it is not always possible to reward a behavior every time it occurs. The student's actions should be rewarded as often as possible, however. Remember, the greater the frequency and amount of the reward, the faster the learning.

the teacher paying attention to him all the time. Having established the desirable behavior, we should now switch to an intermittent reinforcement schedule whereby he is rewarded every now and then for a given desirable behavior, since occasional reinforcement makes behavior persistent and resistant to extinction. Whereas the use of consistent reward is crucial to the learning of behavior, the use of inconsistent reward is crucial to maintaining behavior.

Because teachers often shift from frequent to occasional reward schedules on an intuitive basis, they often use positive reinforcement in an inconsistent haphazard way, thereby undermining its effectiveness. The case of tornado Bill illustrates how a teacher might make decisions about the frequency of rewards on a conscious basis (Hunter, 1967): Tornado Bill, who earned this nickname because of the explosive way he entered the classroom, has been coming in quietly in the morning—from recess, from lunch, from gym class—for the past week. And he has been praised every time, for example, "Good for you, Bill." Bill apparently has learned how to come into the room in the proper way. Hence, now is a good time to switch to irregular rewards so that he will not forget what he has learned. Bill got a hearty reward as he came in for the morning, "Bill, you just never forget to be grown up." After recess, he came in, but the teacher did not reward his quiet entrance as she was busy putting an assignment on the board. He looked a little disappointed because she did not say anything, but he quickly settled down to work. After lunch, when he looked expectantly toward the teacher, he was greeted with "You just don't need a teacher at all. Why even when I'm busy with something else you know what to do!" That was enough reward for that day. The next morning he was greeted again, "Bill, you've come in perfectly all day today without my even looking at you." Before long, Bill was able to get along on even more infrequent rewards and yet maintain his quiet entrances (Hunter, 1967). Note how the teacher "thinned out" the rewards gradually so that she did not impose too lean a schedule of rewards on him too soon. The best recommendation in switching from consistent to inconsistent rewards is to proceed gradually (Neisworth et al., 1969).

The best way to maintain a given behavior at a high level is to reward it on a random or nonsystematic basis. For example, in the above case, the teacher would vary the number of entrances needed to earn a reward. Thus, Bill might not be praised until he had come in properly on four consecutive occasions (4:1), but then he might be praised after only three consecutive acceptable entrances (3:1), and then, perhaps, after six such entrances (6:1), and so on. In this way, Bill would learn that praise is always coming, but he never knows when for sure so that he keeps up the good work hoping that the praise will come this time. To further illustrate this idea, consider the case of maintaining a student's attention during group discussions. If the teacher works her way around the class in a fixed order, first working her way completely through one row and then the next, the students quickly learn that they will be called on (and, hence, have a chance of being rewarded) only once in 30 questions (30:1). Consequently, they quickly lose incentive and engage in inattentive behavior, for example, looking out the window and watching others play. If the teacher varied the order of her questioning, however, and called on students in an unpredictable way, then the student would never know when he might be called on. Hence, he would have to pay close attention.

When Should I Give the Reward?

Timing is especially critical in our giving of rewards. Sometimes teachers give rewards before the child has complied with demands. This is a mistake, since there is little incentive to put forth an effort once the payoff has been received. This is why we customarily pay people *after* they do the job.

How much time should elapse between the performance of the desired behavior and the giving of the reward? Initially, the delay factor may have to be quite short when dealing with acting-out youngsters in that they typically have difficulty postponing gratification. Step by step, however, the interval can be lengthened as the child acquires more adequate behavioral controls. Hence, the teacher initially may have to reward the conduct-disordered child immediately after his good behavior at recess time or in the laboratory. Eventually, if all proceeds well, the student will develop greater ability to postpone gratification. One teacher was able to lengthen the time interval by asking the student if he would mind waiting until tomorrow to get his lifesaver as she was fresh out of them. Another teacher, who had been using art activities for sometime as a potent reward, asked the student if it would be all right if they skipped art this afternoon, since other class activities had run behind schedule.

The delay interval may also have to be short with youngsters whose self-esteem and self-confidence are severely impaired. A seriously disabled reader, for example, may need a reward like the teacher's praise or encouragement immediately after he has sounded out a single word. Later, as he gains in reading skills and personal confidence, he may not need to be rewarded until he has completed a whole page or story. In fact, once the student's frustration tolerance increases, the reward need not even be given during the school day or in the school setting. The accumulations of so many points may be used to earn him a fishing trip with his dad on the weekend or may entitle him to the school picnic that is coming up next month, to watch his favorite TV program that night, or to go horseback riding.

What Type of Reward Should I Use?

Many students—the disorderly as well as the orderly—often become dissatisfied with school by the time that they reach the mid-elementary grades. School life has become a daily grind—a series of obligations to be undertaken without much sense of either extrinsic or intrinsic reward. A large number of students are able to attain the academic objectives set for them, but learning becomes drudgery. Although many students do acquire adequate reading skills, they do not learn to enjoy reading because of their unpleasant experiences in this area. Consequently, they do little reading outside of the educational setting. Probably much of the excitement of learning that youngsters bring to school could be maintained through the careful use of rewards. The writer is not advocating a "fun and games" approach to education. Admittedly, learning must often demand hard work on the student's part. The point to be stressed, however, is that the hard work should be sufficiently rewarding to make the educational process an exciting and personally satisfying experience. Unfortunately, some educators seem to feel that learning should not or cannot be an enjoyable pursuit. If the educational enterprise is to become a personally satisfying and motivating process, educators will most likely need "to turn on" students through the use of various rewards. Many of these rewards initially will be extrinsic in nature, for example, a gold star, some will be intrinsic in nature, for example, patting yourself on the back for doing a good job, and most will eventually involve both, for example, earning your living as a teacher.

In this section our discussion will center around the wide variety of rewards that are available to classroom teachers. For purposes of exposition, rewards will be somewhat arbitrarily divided into the following categories—tangible rewards, social rewards, rewarding activities, and feedback and success experiences. Although they have been described separately, the wise classroom manager will use many different kinds of rewards instead of overworking a single reward to the point that it loses its effectiveness. Even mature adults require the four kinds of reward that we shall discuss.

In deciding on the most suitable reinforcers for the children in question, it is often necessary to consider these factors as developmental level and social-cultural background. What is reinforcing for a lower class child and what is reinforcing for a middle class child may be quite different. Twenty-five cents, for example, might well be motivating to a lower class child but not to an upper middle class child. Similarly, certain rewards may work better with twelve years olds than they do with seven year olds. True enough, there are some things (candy, the teacher's smile, a pat on the back, and the like) which seem to have the status of universal rewards. Even here, however, there are exceptions. The need for caution in this regard is exemplified in research demonstrating that verbal praise is actually aversive for certain emotionally disturbed children (Levin and Simmons, 1962a, 1962b). Thus for some youngsters, praise had a dramatic decelerating influence on the frequency of desirable behavior. This effect is not uncommon among youngsters who hold negative opinions of themselves, since they think the compliment is undeserved and come to distrust the teacher. The negative effects of praise can also occur because the student believes that the particular attribute being complimented is not very important or even bad (for example, a girl doing math). In a similar vein, teacher scolding, while punishing to most students, might prove rewarding to the attention-getting child.

Tangible and Social Rewards. Many psychologists distinguish between social and tangible rewards. Tangible rewards include such things as candy, popcorn, whistles, balloons, stars, trinkets, points, checkmarks, money, and so on. Social rewards, which are rooted in interpersonal relationships, typically include such things as a smile, a wink, verbal and written praise, physical nearness, approval, encouragement, interest, and attention. Because of the unpleasant nature of the earlier associations the disruptive child has had with authority figures, the potency of the teacher as a social reinforcer is not infrequently diminished. Even the teacher's voice through past associations with yelling, nagging, and threatening experiences has often become aversive. In these cases, it is often necessary to begin with tangible or object rewards. These should always be paired, however, with social rewards so that the latter will, through current pleasant association with the tangible rewards, become more potent shapers of behavior in and of themselves. To illustrate, you might say something like, "That's fine, Jim. Let's chalk up another point for you here (tangible reward). I'm sure proud of the way you handled that algebra assignment" (social reward). Eventually we want the student to be capable of responding to verbal and social rewards.

Is there not a danger that the student will become dependent on tangible rewards? Fortunately, this is not the case. First, the teacher gradually takes on greater reward value and this lessens the need for tangible rewards. Her smile, pat on the back, or praise become more powerful than heretofore. Furthermore, the new behaviors have reward power of their own. The disabled reader finds the experience of successful reading very satisfying. The shy child finds a more cooperative way of life a better mode of adjustment. Finally, let us not disparage the use of tangible rewards. Dedicated professionals that we are, we would probably not show up for work if we were not reinforced by dollars—one kind of point system. Furthermore, many a conscientious family man has uprooted his wife and children from their home, church, neighborhood, and friends for two thousand additional points (dollars). Many necessary and desirable societal behaviors are learned and maintained, in part, because of such rewards.

Examples of tangible rewards that teachers have found helpful in changing behavior are given in Table 2.1.

The above discussion is in no way intended to minimize the potency of social rewards, since these rewards are often among the most powerful reinforcers that teachers have at their disposal. Indeed, psychologists have long stressed the importance of teacher warmth and interest. Recent research has confirmed the faith that we have placed in the use of these kinds of social rewards as modifiers of behavior. However, teacher warmth must be applied at the right times and places, that is it must be applied to appropriate behaviors. Merely increasing the amount of teacher warmth (smiles, words of praise, encouragement, understanding, and the like) will not result in more acceptable behavior when it is handed out in an indiscriminate fashion. Teacher warmth, like any other kind of reward, must be earned and attached to the child's specific actions that we wish to strengthen. Love is not enough. Remember that social rewards often can come from sources other than the teacher. A sample list of social rewards is presented in Table 2.2.

Activity Rewards and the Reinforcement Menu. Activities can also be used as rewards. Teachers can identify a variety of rewarding events by simply asking students what activities they enjoy, through the observation of activities enjoyed by students, or by estimating how much time students might spontaneously spend in activities when no restrictions are made on their behavior. Having identified a number of rewarding activities, the teacher then makes access to these preferred activities contingent on participation in less preferred activities. For example, you might notice that a given student who typically does not complete math assignments (a loathsome and low-frequency activity) will build electronic gadgets whenever an opportunity exists (a preferred and high-frequency behavior). At this point, you may make a contractual agreement with the student which states that if he completes his math assignment, he then

TABLE 2.1

Tangible Rewards

Balloons

Toys (slinkie, bubble blowers, model airplanes)

Stars (on forehead)

Points

Checkmarks

Use of stamps or stickers (old Christmas seals or magazine stamps)

Educational puzzles

Rubber stamps of animal pictures

Plastic multicolored rings which lock together and can be used to make necklaces and chains or can be used for purchases in the school store

Tokens

A band on child's desk with objects to be colored; for every row of completed assignment, the child could color one object (animals, cars, circus persons, etc.)

Ribbon awards. These can be specially fitted (The Winnie the Pooh Award—for the quietest student, The Christopher Robin Hood Work Award, The Courtesy Award)

Money given by parents over and above the student's allowance

Raisins, popcorn, apples, milk, marshmallows

Baseball cards

Comics

Going to drinking fountain without permission

The use of teacher's staplers, magic markers and paper punch in some personal project

The use of the punching bag

The use of the typewriter

Magazines (*Hot Rod, Seventeen, Playboy, Sports Illustrated, Popular Mechanics*)

Athletic passes

Tickets to swimming pool

Access to weights for body building

Use of view master

Special passes

Pinball machine to play

Door key for delinquent boys in correctional institutions

Buttons with current rage sayings

Teacher's tie—boy admired teacher's tie; could wear it on Friday if behaved during the week

Teacher's sunglasses—could wear them out to the playground and back into the classroom during recess period

Swimming cap: girl could earn one if she would enter pool and learn how to swim

Use of popular music and hearing own special records (earphones)

Bringing in favorite "personality posters" to put up in place of instructor's own pictures

TABLE 2.2

Social Rewards

Approval and recognition from authority figures such as parents, teachers, counselors,
principals, patrol guards, custodians

Communicating respect ("Your answer was clever"; "Nobody else thought of that"; "Jim, your explanation was crystal clear"; "Clarence, it's a pleasure having you in class when you work like this").

Friendliness, warmth (walking with student; putting your hand on student's shoulder; smiling; announcing student's birthday).

Putting name of students on the board for the most improved behavior or good behavior.

Nonverbal social rewards (patting head, ruffling hair, winking, touching hand).

Have parent or principal sign good papers.

Take Polaroid pictures of student, placing his picture in frame for "The Most Improved Student of the Week."

Express interest both verbally and written on his papers. Use of humor, "in-group" or currently popular expressions such as "Zowey," "Bravo," "Neato," "A-O.K.," "Wow," "Fantastic!!," "Terrific!!," "Delightful," "Nifty," "Fabulous!," "Exciting!!," "Show this to your parents" (these could also be used for feedback purposes).

Children given double A's for accomplishments such as neatest papers, attention during reading period, behavior problem improvement, and the like. The children are allowed to see their marks at any time.

Smiling Sam: a smiling face for good papers; a smiling face with a wink for papers needing improvement; and a frowning face for unacceptable work.

Have special rewards available on Mondays and Fridays so that the school week opens and closes on a pleasant note.

Early dismissal—either from school to be first in line for busses or before lunch.

Pick the teacher as a playmate for a game.

A note of good behavior sent to parents.

If the disorderly child got through one half of the day successfully, the teacher gave him a note so stating to take to the principal, who placed the commendation in a frame with his picture.

Placing the child's name on the board for desirable behavior; teacher could have a special place on the board for "Names of the Behavers."

Have parents or someone of student's choice invited to visit the classroom.

Responsibility and authority

Can feed and take home over weekend class pets (rabbits, parakeets, ant farm, turtles, hamsters).

Can be first in line, could have an added designation with either titles or props ("The Door Man," "The White Hat Child," "The Sheriff.")

Be stage manager for a class play.

For physical education:
    Don't dress for class—be a coach.

TABLE 2.2 (cont.)

Be assistant referee.

Take an early shower.

Check showers, supplies, and equipment.

Be bathroom supervisor at the end of recess.

Be attendance taker for coming to school on time.

Being allowed to sit in teacher's chair.

Correcting papers after finishing assignment.

Being allowed to be the class librarian for the day.

Being able to give the practice spelling test.

Reward for poor reader in the upper grades to go to the first grade to read or write stories for them as a tutor.

Making up a geometry (or subject area) quiz, administering it to the rest of the class, and then scoring and grading it. Student would receive a grade for the job.

Appear as guest lecturer in other classes.

Choosing the extra credit problems for the week and determining how they will affect the students' grade

Approval from peer group

Express interest in him and his improved behavior.

Can go on overnights with class.

Can be member of class council.

Class project for cooperation is to work on class newspaper. Reward for participation is being voted "Reporter of the week": "Photographer of the month," etc.

"Home movies" made of class activities.

"Who's Who Club"—All the girls in the class belong to the club, and can only keep their membership by displaying a well-behaved manner at all times. They were allowed to have various types of activities.

Citizenship award.

Let a student who has been "good" place the stars on his classmates "A" papers.

can pursue his interest in electronics for a specified period of time. Initially, the disliked activity and the enjoyable activity are scheduled back to back. Thus, as soon as he has completed his assignment to your satisfaction, he gains access to preferred activities. Later on, it may be possible to schedule the activity for the last part of the school day. Research evidence indicates that low probability behaviors, for example, doing math lessons, increase in frequency by making the more rewarding pursuits contingent on prior performance. Apart from its simplicity and flexibility, this approach has the advantage of allowing the teacher to use activities that are a natural part of the typical classroom schedule. Examples of activities used to change classroom behavior are provided in Table 2.3.

TABLE 2.3

Activities As Rewards

Listen to Radio Moscow and Radio Cuba on the teacher's shortwave radio using earphones—then discussing of other's perception on Vietnam War.

Extension or inclusion of enjoyable classroom activities such as gym, art, music, recess.

Paper folding (origami), which each child contributed to main class mobile.

Making charts for tournament play (physical education).

Making "spirit" signs for upcoming athletic event to hang in the halls (physical education).

Killing or catching flies for feeding live animals in the classroom.

Play tic-tac-toe with colored chalk on the blackboard.

Catching grasshoppers during last 5 minutes of class to feed frogs and fish (general science class).

"Surprise sack"—reaching into sack for a small token or slip telling of special activity.

Choose your own seat in the room.

Arm wrestle.

Reading a library book.

Writing notes if this does not disrupt classroom activity.

Taking off shoes and walking barefooted.

Rocking in the rocking chair.

Drawing pictures at desk.

Daydreaming.

Studying other subjects.

Putting head down and resting.

Doing crosswords provided in the classroom.

Card tricks: a youngster who knew a card trick could teach others.

Students were allowed to listen to stories on tape recorder enclosed in a stall at the back of the classroom. They could select the story they wanted or take a chance by listening to the tape already on the machine.

During nap time, the child is allowed to play with a toy instead of putting it away, e.g. girls—dolls, beads; boys—trucks, jets.

The privilege of being allowed to go outside to draw.

"Super reward"—a picture of the teacher or principal is hung on the back wall, and the student is allowed to throw darts at the picture.

Challenging the instructor or another student to a game of chess (or any other game).

Play hang-man.

Sharpen pencils.

Even the window shades.

Clean the erasers.

Turn the lights on and off.

TABLE 2.3 (cont.)

Sweep the room.

Put the shelves in order.

Being able to attend other subject area classes *for the group.*

Having a supervised snow ball fight.

"Gripe day"—on specified day the students can select a gripe they want to discuss. The topics can include anything, except other teachers.

Have a supervised class Tug of War.

Having a box lunch auction—especially for 5th and 6th graders.

Spelling B's.

Chewing gum.

Allowing the children to move their desks and use the area to dance.

Having a panel discussion of current topic or current event discussions on Fridays (dress codes, use of drugs, dropping out of school, "the generation gap").

Holding class outdoors on warm, sunny days.

Playing "Stump the teacher" game.

Spot talent shows—children entertain class.

Field trips:

    Zoo, farm, community agencies.

    Tickets to major football or baseball game.

    Visit to the university.

    Going to a restaurant.

Hobbies that the student has.

It is generally a good idea to give the student a voice in his choice of rewards. To this end, the reinforcement menu has been devised (Addison and Homme, 1966). The reinforcement menu consists of a list of rewarding activities from which the student can choose once he has completed his assigned task. For young students or for those who have reading handicaps, the menu can be presented in a pictorial format. By allowing the student to select his reward from the menu, one is able to determine precisely the most effective reinforcer for him at that point in time. Herein lies the beauty of the menu. Examples of reinforcement menus for children of varying grade levels are presented in Tables 2.4, 2.5, and 2.6.

Homme (1969) makes the following instructive comments regarding the use of reinforcement menus in the classroom:

    1. Some activities on the menu are purely entertaining, but others are educational as well as entertaining. High priority should be

TABLE 2.4

Reinforcement Menu: Kindergarten

Main Courses
1. Playing piano
2. Using puppets for a puppet show
3. Painting
4. Looking out the window
5. Using the toys at back of room
6. Working with puzzles
7. Using play-dough
8. Moving chair to another part of the room
9. Drawing
10. Playing favorite game
11. Cutting and pasting
12. Talking to a classmate
13. Drinking
14. Hugging
15. Using colored chalk
16. Swinging feet
17. Walking around in back of the room
18. Cupcake party
19. Watch David and Goliath on television
20. Singing

Daily Specials[a]
Monday. Visit first grade
Tuesday. Finger painting
Wednesday. Using teacher as a playmate in a game
Thursday. Make a mural
Friday. Listen to stories or records using earphones

[a] Many teachers prefer to have "specials" just two or three times per week.

given to the reinforcing activities that relate to educational objectives.

2. In selecting reinforcing activities, attention should be given to three criteria—the availability of the rewards in the school, the noise level, and the response level of the students to the activities. Although items can sometimes be brought from home if they are not available in the classroom, preference ordinarily is given to activities that are a more natural part of the educational setting. Since some students will still be working while others are enjoying a rewarding activity, quiet activities are often preferred over noisy ones. Students generally tire of items on the menu after awhile, so that it becomes

TABLE 2.5

Reinforcement Menu: Elementary Class

1. Go to the library to work on a special project relating to the unit being studied.
2. Arrange the game shelf and being permitted to pick out a game to play.
3. Listen to the reading stories on the phonograph with earphones (up to four at a time).
4. The use of the electric and flannel board to work on exercises found in the science corner.
5. Work in the art corner or take out plain paper and draw any kind of pictures at desk.
6. Record favorite story on the tape recorder making sure that it is read with expression and clarity.
7. Work on scrapbook on history project—can use the magazines in the room.
8. Leave five minutes early for lunch.
9. Be line captain.
10. Be in charge of taking attendance.
11. Can get a drink at any time without asking permission.
12. Be in charge of passing out papers and other class materials.
13. Be excused 15 minutes early before the end of the school day to clean the erasers and blackboard.
14. Let teams of students wad up spitballs, throw them at the wastebasket, and see which has the best record.
15. Permitting students to draw on steamed-up windows with their fingers.

Specials

Monday. Listen to the transistor radio via earphones.

Tuesday. Use of the viewmaster to look at pictures of the country being studied in geography.

Wednesday. Be group leader for the social studies group.

Thursday. Add another piece to the classroom puzzle or mural.

Friday. Plan for the Friday afternoon group activity—help the teacher pick out the group game to be played.

necessary to change items periodically and to inform the students of these changes.

3. If possible, the teacher should devise a "reinforcement area" and a "task area." Ideally these two areas should be separated. If separation is not possible, students can pursue rewarding activities of a quiet nature (coloring, reading, checkers, and the like) at their desk. Quiet background music helps if too much noise is generated as a consequence of having the reinforcement area in the same classroom as the task area. In short, the teacher can select one of three

TABLE 2.6

Reinforcement Menu: High School Geometry Class

1. Challenging teacher or another student to a game of chess.
2. Using the portable computer.
3. Doing extra credit problems and seeing how they can raise his grade.
4. Making up a geometry quiz and then giving it to the class.
5. Sitting at the teacher's desk while doing homework problems.
6. Preparing the bulletin board using a display of the student's choice.
7. Writing letters.
8. Playing chess.
9. Reading.
10. Playing charades.
11. Talking over past or forthcoming athletic or social events.
12. Having a creative exhibit period (a grown-up version of show-and-tell).
13. Comparing a 1902 Sears-Roebuck catalogue with the current one, discussing changes in style, price, and the like, and trying to discover why the changes occurred.

Daily Specials

Monday. Appear as guest lecturer in the other math classes.

Tuesday. Do the special crossword puzzles involving geometry concepts learned.

Wednesday. Time in which you can play a math game with another student.

Thursday. Construction of special paper models using geometrical figures to complete.

Friday. Do mystery problems involving mathematical solutions.

---

alternatives—using a separate room, dividing the classroom, or using the student's desk.

4. How long should the student spend on any given activity? There are various methods for answering this question. One can simply prespecify the amount of time, for example, five minutes. One also can base the amount of time on the level of mastery or on the difficulty of the task. Finally, one could use a procedure that involves chance to determine the amount of time, for example, rolling dice. In general, Homme believes that the time limit should not be less than three minutes nor more than ten. If more time is used, there is a danger that the reinforcing event might lose some of its reward value. On the other hand, if less than three minutes is given, the student really does not have enough time to enjoy the activity.[3]

---

[3] Teachers will find that the length of time depends, in part, on the student in

5. A final consideration is concerned with the methods of controlling the time spent in the reinforcement area. Among the possibilities are "sign—in/out sheet," timing devices, peer pressure, or having students leave the area when the minute hand hits the five-minute indicator. If the student has to work at his desk, he might wear a colored card while he pursues the rewarding activity, or some other signal system might be devised.

Feedback and Success Experience as Intrinsic Rewards. It is important that we let the student know how he is progressing, since feedback can serve as a source of reward. Although feedback can be provided verbally, for example, "Jim, that's just fine," we can report progress in a more objective and, perhaps, in a more motivating way if some kind of a record is kept. One type of chart is shown in Table 2.7.

Other kinds of charts used by teachers include the following.

Number of books read—draw in another book on the "library book shelf" chart.

"Monkey climbing coconut tree" to reach candy coconut (increments depend on number of spelling words had correct).

Race track competition (move assigned car for each assignment or book completed).

Baseball diamonds (runners advance from base to base).

Football fields (runner moves toward opponent's end zone).

Sound trains (used in speech correction).

Bank account (each student has an account of $500 from which he could have deposits or withdrawals according to behavior).

Jogging chart.

Success experiences also provide a very important source of reward. Although extrinsic rewards may often have to be relied on heavily during the early part of a behavior modification program, they should be gradually replaced, in part, by rewards that are intrinsic to the desirable activity. The passive student learns to enjoy self-assertion, the disabled reader finds joy in becoming competent, the high school dropout thrives on achieving a sense of mastery. Indeed, the overcoming of problems or handicaps is frequently rewarding in and of itself. There are many ways

question and on the activity. For example, some students can work for extended periods of time on activities of educational value without becoming bored with them.

TABLE 2.7

Behavioral Chart

Name:

Rule:

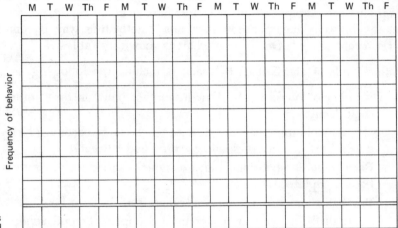

in which teachers have relied on mastery and curiosity motives in modifying behavior. Examples are provided in Table 2.8.

In conclusion, the shift away from reward by others and tangible objects toward intrinsic reward is central to the student's progress toward self-management—our ultimate objective.

WHAT IF DESIRABLE BEHAVIOR DOES NOT OCCUR?

One problem which crops up is the student's failure to display rewardable behavior. The teacher cannot reinforce acceptable behavior when there is none. There must be something to reward. In many instances

TABLE 2.8

Rewards Stemming from a Sense of Mastery and Accomplishment or from
Academic Activities

Taking pride in one's achievement

Winning a dictionary (25 cents) by recognizing and circling most words in a maze of letters.

Writing creative short stories with the addition that the children are allowed to interrupt and to ask the correct spelling of difficult words.

An exercise involving sentences. One half of a sentence is written by the teacher, the student finishes the sentence (the only requirement is that the sentence must make sense).

If all daily assignments are handed in for the marking period, dismissing students from last test, and giving them a grade of 100.

Have teacher aide read to student or having students read to teacher aide.

The use of a tape recorder. Permitting students to talk into it and listen to their voices. (This exercise is used to encourage listening and language.)

Timing math assignment with a three-minute egg timer—"Beat the timer."

Letting students do old worksheets.

Solving mysteries in which the solution is based on various points of word usage.

Letting a child with desirable behavior have a portion of the bulletin board to put up whatever he wants.

Being able to control and delay gratification

For the hyperactive youngster a reward might be just walking around the room for a certain amount of time.

For specified amount of time in his seat, a child can be given a piece of the whole puzzle. On completion of the puzzle, he is given a choice of rewards.

When a child exhibits a new behavior that you have been trying to elicit from him, use a "home movie" camera to take 15 to 20 seconds of footage of this child exhibiting the desired behavior. This could be used for later child-teacher conferences or the child could see his "footage" during free time.

Increased curiosity: "doing something novel"

Use slides, especially in an area of interest.

Use microscope (swamp water for blank slides and prepared slides are available).

Work with geology kit (the student is assigned an unknown rock, and he performs tests at his desk to identify the rock).

---

there would be an endless wait if rewards were restricted to only perfect performance. In everyday practice, it is more effective to reward approximations of the desired behavior, that is, to reward small steps in the right direction. Gradually, the student must perform more and more steps in the right direction before the reward is given. At the outset, for example, it may be necessary to reward a disabled reader after he recognizes the letters in a given word. Gradually as his skills improve, he will be expected to recognize words before being rewarded. Then we might demand that he complete a sentence, a paragraph, a page, or a whole lesson in order to earn his reward. We must always remember to reward improvement.

A good rule to follow is to *start small* and to reward the first signs of appropriate behavior. In the beginning, it is best to set low requirements for earning a reward. Consider the youngster who refuses to complete arithmetic assignments even though the instruction is geared to his level. The teacher might reward him for the following successive approximations or improvements:

1. Being in his seat even though he is not working.
2. Taking out his arithmetic book.
3. Opening the book to the assignment.
4. Looking at it.
5. Picking up his pencil.
6. Doing one problem.
7. Doing two or three problems.
8. Doing a short row of problems.
9. Doing the two rows of addition problems.
10. Doing the two rows of subtraction problems.
11. Completing the arithmetic assignment.
12. Finally completing the assignment at higher levels of accuracy.

On each of these occasions, rewards should be given for his approximations of the ultimate performance required. For example, on noticing him looking at the assignment, the teacher might say in a pleasant tone, "Good, I'm glad to see you've got the right book today and that you're ready to go." Eventually, rewards will be given only when the student completes his assignment satisfactorily. Notice that the successful completion of this sequence must be undertaken over a period of time. Hence, guard against the tendency to expect too rapid a change. Also remember that the steps appropriate for one youngster may be either too large or too small for other activities or for other students. With the negativistic child, we might want to start with situations in which he is generally cooperative (for example, sending him on an errand) and gradually introduce those situations in which he is uncooperative. Since cooperative behavior is a habit he has yet to acquire, rewards must be given as often as possible in this situation. One hundred percent reinforcement would be ideal. By rewarding his cooperative efforts, we are strengthening behavior that competes with negativistic behavior. The student cannot do both at the same time. If the student fails to become more cooperative, consideration should be given to the use of smaller steps and of more rewards in the shaping process. Increasing incentives is another way of facilitating the onset of desired behavior that we want to reward. Increasing the payoff makes the teacher's way of doing things more attractive to the student and thus increases the probability that he will engage in the behavior we seek. Even mature adults generally will perform activities that they dislike if the price is right. Modeling procedures (especially guided participation) and punishment can also be used in cases where it is difficult initially to elicit desirable behavior for the purposes of reinforcement. These last two techniques will be discussed in more detail later.

REWARDS AND RULES

All teachers use rules in their attempts at classroom management. For our purposes, we shall define a rule as any task the student must perform, or as any decision regarding what he may or may not do.[4] A good rule should have three properties. It must be definable, reasonable, and enforceable (Smith and Smith, 1966). Rather than tell a student, "From here on in, you behave yourself in my class," it would be better if the teacher spelled out one or two specific rules to guide the student's conduct. For instance, the teacher might state, "You are to work on your algebra assignment for the rest of this period. There will be no talking during this time." Rules can also be unreasonable at times. The teacher might, for example, expect the student to accomplish a task for which his skills are deficient or for which the time limits are too demanding. Finally, if a rule cannot be enforced, through rewards and/or punishments, it will be ineffective in guiding behavior. Basically, people are consequence seekers. That is, we try to find out what will happen if we do comply with a given request and what will happen if we do not comply.

[4] There are three questions that a teacher should ask about the disorderly student. (1) Does he know what is expected of him, that is, does he clearly understand what the rules are? Directions can appear crystal clear to the teacher, but the information they provide to the students might well be incomplete, inaccurate, or conflicting. If there is confusion about the ground rules, it is then necessary to make them as explicit as possible. Listing the rules on the board, having the student explain in his own words what the rule means, minimizing distractions while giving the directions, and keeping rules brief are all ways in which the student can be helped to understand the rules. The teacher also should be careful to relate the student's behavior to the rule so that

Teachers often invite difficulty by establishing unnecessary and impractical rules. One sage strategy, therefore, is to start with a limited number of rules. With extremely unsocialized youngsters, it might be best to start with just one rule. Which rule (s) should be selected? One that will most effectively promote significant academic and personal skills in the child, one that is of major concern to you as a teacher and, definitely, one that is enforceable. A rule forbidding chewing gum would probably not be a good one with which to start. Although well defined, it is difficult to enforce as the student can swallow it or chew it when you are not looking. Furthermore, compliance with this rule does little to develop important scholastic or social achievements. It would be better to state that the student must complete satisfactorily a given assignment before he can turn to other activities that he enjoys. This rule would be clear, enforceable, and beneficial.

There are several reasons why we should start with a very small number of rules. Foremost among them are the following.

1. Too many rules amount to nagging. Students feel that the teacher is always on them—if not for one thing, then for another.

2. If the teacher has been inconsistent in the past, the students' testing of this first rule will be more intense and prolonged than for later rules. Briefly, enforcement of your first rules will probably demand all the energy you can summon. When the students learn that you are firm and mean business, there will be less testing of later rules.

he knows exactly for what he is being rewarded or punished (for example, "Now, you're *paying attention*"). (2) If the student knows the rules but still misbehaves, then you should consider the second question, namely, does he have the skills and abilities to do what I asked him to accomplish? Much misbehavior probably occurs as a result of demands that exceed the student's current level of readiness. When behavior problems stem from skill deficits and are secondary to the learning problem, it is necessary to teach the academic and social skills needed to assume the role of a student. The five techniques discussed in this book should help teachers to overcome deficits in the skill area. The provision of greater freedom of choice regarding curriculum also deserves serious consideration in these cases. One high school, for instance, listed more than fifty different English and social studies courses from which the students could choose. In short, one can change the student and/or change his environment to better suit his present skills by gearing instructions to his abilities and interests. (3) When the student knows what the rules are and when he has the competencies to perform in an acceptable way, and yet continues to misbehave, then we must ask a third question: Is he motivated to do what is expected of him? On many occasions the disruptive student finds his deviant ways more satisfying than conventional ways. In these cases, we must increase the reward value of the school setting so that students move toward it instead of away from it or strike out at it. The techniques presented in the chapters that follow are also relevant to the solution of motivational problems.

3. Students often will focus their misbehavior on established rules. Other kinds of misbehavior may be abandoned as students concentrate their energies on breaking the few rules you have established. This knowledge is useful. By selecting a rule you know to be enforceable, you have at your disposal a clear plan by which consequences can be implemented. This is one way of stacking the deck in your favor.

4. Finally, you will see that there is a change in the classroom following the enforcement of only a few rules. This change in behavior will lessen the need for rules that earlier seemed warranted (Smith and Smith, 1966).

An interesting study by Madsen, Becker, and Thomas (1968) investigated the separate effects of rules, ignoring inappropriate behaviors and the approval for appropriate behavior. During the rules phase, the teacher developed four or five rules, posted them on a chart, and went over them three or four times daily, asking the students to repeat them. The rules included instructions such as, "Sit quietly while working," "Raise your hand," and the like. Although it seems reasonable to believe that just telling students what is expected should have a desirable impact on their conduct, this was not found to be the case. Rules alone had little impact on classroom behavior. The combination of showing approval for appropriate behavior and of ignoring inappropriate behavior, however, did prove very effective in promoting more acceptable classroom behavior. Giving approval for appropriate behavior, in of itself, also resulted in better classroom conduct. The authors concluded that rules must be made (and can be made) a significant force in classroom management by having teachers provide reinforcement for student compliance with rules. Viewed in this perspective, rules become a necessary but not sufficient condition for acceptable behavior. There must be a payoff. Furthermore, as will be evident from the discussion in the next section, it is often wise to involve the peer group in the formation of classroom guidelines.

In summary, it would be well to remember the following guidelines for establishing rules[5] (Madsen and Madsen, 1970).

1. Be sure to involve the class in making up the rules.
2. Rules should be short and to the point.
3. Try to phrase the rules in a positive way.
4. Call attention to the rules at times other than when someone has misbehaved.

[5] These guidelines seem most applicable to the elementary school level.

5. Rules should differ for varied activities.
6. Let the student know when the different rules are in effect.
7. Post the rules in a conspicuous location and review regularly.
8. Keep a personal record of the number of times that you review the rules.

THE PEER GROUP AND REWARDS

The teacher is not the sole source of reward. Nor is he always the primary source of reward in the classroom. The effective classroom manager realizes these facts of classroom life and will make use of other sources of rewards, for instance, the peer group. In many instances, the teacher will have at his disposal a ready tool in peer group support because other students are often annoyed by unacceptable behavior and are as anxious as the teacher to have it cleared up. Group praise, recognition, and rejection, although commonly overlooked as a method of classroom management, can be very effective tools for the building and maintaining of desirable behavior. Although students are always concerned about what their peers think of them, the susceptibility to peer influence is relatively minimal during the preschool years, reaches a peak during middle childhood, and tends to decrease with the onset of adolescence.

One study that demonstrated the potency of the peer group as modifiers of troublesome behavior was conducted in a class for educationally handicapped elementary school students (Stiavelli and Shirley, 1968). In this study, the Citizenship Council (CC), a group procedure that used group pressure and positive rewards, was established in an effort to lighten the teacher's disciplinary burden. Pupils met each day at 12:30 P.M. to nominate and to vote on which students had earned or had lost their citizenship on the basis of their performance on the playground, in the cafeteria, and in the classroom. The class, teacher, and the two aides met as a group and established by unanimous vote the criteria for citizenship, rewards, privileges, and disciplinary consequences. The following four lists were established.

I. Rules of Conduct for Citizenship—A Citizen
   1. Respects the rights of others.
   2. Respects the property of others.
   3. Hands in assignments on time.
   4. Does not tattle.

5. Does unto others as he would have them do unto him.
6. Does all his work neatly and accurately.
7. Raises his hand to talk or ask a question and does not interrupt others.
8. Lines up quietly.
9. Helps others.
10. Tries to understand others' behavior.

II. Rewards

1. A gold pin with the inscription "Citizenship." (The principal pinned on the pin the first time earned and the student was allowed to take the pin home to show his parents. Thereafter, he was pinned by the teacher and kept it through the school day.)

2. A gold plaque with the inscription "Citizen of the Month." (This was given to the student who had received the most stars on the progress chart and was hung in the student's cubicle.)

3. A gold star. (This was placed on the progress chart for each day of citizenship earned. The students were acutely aware of the chart and it proved to be an effective reinforcer.)

III. Privileges

1. The citizens are to be allowed to go and come from the room to the lavatory or for a drink and to move about the room as they wish without asking for permission as the noncitizens are required to do. The citizen is only required to inform the teacher or aides as to what he plans to do or where he is going.

2. The citizens are to be allowed to leave for lunch five minutes earlier than the noncitizens. (This placed them first in the cafeteria line and out on the playground five minutes early.)

3. During recess and P.E. the citizens are to be allowed first choice of playground equipment and be first in line to go out and come into the room.

4. Only the citizens are to be chosen as class helpers and messengers.

5. The citizen of the month and his two closest competitors on the progress chart are to be taken bowling during school hours. (One game lasting approximately one hour).

IV. Disciplinary Measures

    1. A spanking of two to five swats administered by the principal.

    2. Loss of citizenship for an extended period of time, with a maximum of two weeks.

    3. Isolation during lunch, P.E., and recess either in the room or in principal's office.

Observations made by school personnel indicated the effectiveness of this technique. Group cohesiveness increased, the students' frustration tolerance rose, self-control improved, and teaching became more enjoyable. Interestingly, the parents of a neurologically handicapped child, although initially opposed to this group process, became its staunchest defenders as their son's behavior improved both at school and at home. One caution to bear in mind with the use of this technique is that the tendency of peers is to be too severe in setting standards for behavior. It is, perhaps, wise to suggest a trial period before drafting a more permanent set of guidelines, since initial guidelines are generally too demanding to live with comfortably for an extended period of time.

Another application of the use of the group for managing behavior is the "Social-Problem Solving Meeting" (Glasser, 1961). Students are seated in a circle and individual as well as group problems are discussed. The problems for discussion can be proposed by the students, the teacher, the principal, or the counselor. These meetings are conducted once a week or as the situation warrants. The meetings are designed to give students an active voice in the finding of solutions for individual or group problems. Discussions are to be held in a constructive, nonjudgmental way, without faultfinding or punishment. Glasser, a psychiatrist, reports when students discover that their classmates do care about them (a social reward), they can make intelligent plans for solving disciplinary problems. This approach might prove even more effective in changing behavior if guidelines for behavior were charted and enforced through the use of rewards and punishment.

The effectiveness of peer group reinforcement also receives support in the work of Patterson and Anderson (1964), Hartup (1964), and Titkin and Hartup (1965). What is surprising, at first glance, is the suggestion that approval from a disliked or unpopular peer has greater reward value than does approval from a liked peer. Teachers, however, have long recognized that having two friends work together often interferes with the completion of a given task or assignment. Students are apparently challenged more by peers who are negatively perceived than by close friends. The teacher, therefore, might do well to have the disorderly student sit at a table with nonfriends for, at least, certain assignments or during troublesome times of the day, for example, late afternoon when his ability to resist temptation is lowered. The peers at his table could easily be taught to reward his academic and/or social progress.

There is little question that teachers need to make more effective use of group dynamics is promoting the social and academic adjustment of their students. To facilitate self-control on the student's part, the teacher must reduce dependence on himself and must offer the class opportunities for self-management. Classroom management should not and need not be the responsibility of the teacher alone. This is especially true at the secondary level when students feel a need for greater self-determination. The teacher who arbitrarily and unilaterally imposes standards in a high-handed fashion is inviting trouble (Kaplan, 1970). On the other hand, a cohesive group with a high degree of morale can go far in preventing disciplinary problems. A teacher cannot afford to ignore the power and persuasiveness of the group in establishing and enforcing class rules.

CONTINGENCY CONTRACTS

The notion of establishing a form of contractual agreement between the student and the teacher was mentioned previously in the discussion on activity rewards. The basic rationale of the contingency contract is that "you can do something pleasant, if you perform this task." Homme (1969) states that much of the essence of contingency contracting has been captured in Grandma's Law—"first clean up your plate, then you may have your dessert." In the school setting, the contract specifies that the student can engage in an enjoyable high preference task, for example, art activities, or will receive a very desirable tangible or social reward, if he first engages in a low preference task, for example, a math assignment. To be effective, the contract must offer a reward that is (a) highly attractive, and (b) not obtainable outside the conditions of the contract (Homme, 1969). Educators have utilized this technique for years, but they have not made the terms of the contract explicit, nor have they used contracts systematically. Educational contracts, while useful with elementary school students, are especially effective at the secondary level in that they enhance the adolescent's development of responsibility and yet permit some freedom to choose his goals and rewards.

Homme (1969), who has done extensive work in this area, lists three basic types of contracts depending on whether the terms are set by a manager, the student himself, or by both. In manager-controlled contracting, the manager determines the amount of the reward, establishes the amount of the task to be accomplished, presents the contract to the student (which he accepts), and delivers the reward. This kind of contracting is quite different from self-contracting in which the student himself determines the amount of the task and the amount of the reward. Self-contracting, however, is usually the last of the three types of contracts entered into, since it demands self-control and initiative on the student's part. In leading the student from manager (teacher)—controlled contracts to self-contracting, it is often necessary to use what is called transitional contracting in which the teacher and student jointly decide on the amount of reinforcement and on the magnitude of the task.

Homme (1969) cautions that the contract should be revised when one or more of the following occurs.

1. Incomplete assignments.
2. Complaining.
3. Excessive dawdling.
4. Talking and wasting time.
5. Excessive clock watching.
6. Inattention to instructions or details.
7. Failure to pass more than two progress checks in one subject area.

Sometimes it is necessary to shorten the contract by deleting certain terms or by simplifying the required tasks. If this strategy fails, the teacher might suspect that the rewards are not sufficiently enticing. At times, it may be necessary to lengthen the contract by increasing the number of tasks or their difficulty. On these occasions, it may also be necessary to increase the amount of reward to make the harder assignments more worthwhile. It is important that the student be made to feel that he has achieved a new status, for example, "Jim, you've improved so much that you're now ready for the advanced material." More will be said about the use of educational contracts when we discuss punishment procedures in the next chapter.

Table 2.9 presents a transitional contract for a 16-year-old student who seldom completed homework assignments in his social studies class. In general, he reacted to his teacher's comments in a negative and sullen manner.

EXAMPLES OF REWARDS

Problem: Class was not doing seatwork
Reward: A game

Reading time proved troublesome for a first-year teacher. Her prime concern centered on the low study rate of pupils who were at their desks

TABLE 2.0

Educational Contract

Between (Student's name) and (Teacher's name)

Student agrees to:

1. Complete assigned homework—if well done and accurate	5 points 2 extra points
2. Hand in assignments on date due—if handed in before due date	5 points 2 extra points

Teacher agrees to:

1. Check homework and give appropriate amount of points to the student (as indicated above).

2. Not reprimand or comment when homework is not completed or handed in.

   (a) if two consecutive assignments are not handed in—3 points are subtracted from accumulated total.

   (b) if three consecutive assignments are not completed and handed in the contract is considered void.

Student can exchange his points for:

(1) Free period time during class (5 points per 5 minutes)

(2) Access to the driving range (10 points per 15 minutes)

(3) Excuse from the weekly Social Studies quiz (30 points each week)

(4) Being helper to shop teacher (10 points per 15 minutes)

(5) Credits for purchase of pocket book (5 points per credit—10 credits for free book)

(6) Being a student referee for a varsity game (30 points per game)

(7) Access to student lounge during free period (study hall) (30 points per period)

Signed ———————————————
                              Student

Signed ———————————————
                              Teacher

---

doing seatwork while she was working with small groups in a reading circle at the front of the room. At the start of this study, the average study rate of pupils at their desks was 51 percent. As a result of her paying greater attention to the students, study rose to 62 percent. But the teacher still was not satisfied. Therefore, a "study game" was introduced as a reward for an appropriate seatwork. Many teachers know this game as "7 Up"—a game in which the teacher selects the seven best studiers to go to the front of the class. The rest of the class then put their heads down on the desks and shut their eyes. The seven tiptoe around and touch one of the seated students on the head. The seated pupils then have to guess who touched them. If they guess correctly, they go to the front of the room and are "it" next time. This game was renamed so that its relationship to study behavior would be clear. This game is a favorite among elementary school pupils and can be used in the ordinary classroom. By having the "Study Game" follow the reading period and contingent on the effective use of their time spent in seatwork, the study rate rose to about 80 percent. These results were especially satisfying because they were achieved in the last week of school—a time when students are particularly rambunctious (Hall et al., 1968).

Comment. It is interesting to notice that positive reinforcement can be used effectively with groups as well as with a given individual student. This observation is especially significant, since the teacher is first and foremost a group worker. Also instructive is the finding that this technique can be used to good advantage by a beginning teacher. Indeed, the systematic use of positive reinforcement may well have saved her job.

This study also illustrates the use of an activity as a reward to be given only after students had made effective use of their time spent in seatwork. The students had more fun in school and yet made better use of their school time.

•   •   •

Problem: Poor achievement in arithmetic

Reward: An interesting object

One first grade teacher made excellent use of a Mickey Mouse watch as a reward in "reaching" Tom, who refused to go near a math worksheet. The teacher capitalized on his fascination with her Mickey Mouse watch. She struck a bargain (contract) with him. If he would let her help him with his arithmetic for ten minutes, he could actually wear the watch for five minutes. Given this "foot in the door," it was not too long before he began to develop interest and skill in math.

Comment. One of the best ways to discover what is rewarding for a given youngster is to take note of his interests. Although this sounds easy enough, many teachers probably would have overlooked the potential significance of Tom's interest in the Mickey Mouse watch and would not have capitalized on it in their efforts to teach him math. Also note the use of the educational contract.

•   •   •

Problem: Nonreader

Reward: Allowing him to pursue his interest in piano

George, an emotionally disturbed student, was introduced to reading through his interest in the piano. He could help the teacher play the piano provided that he completed his reading assignment satisfactorily. She also related his interest in the piano to his reading assignments. First, a song that he liked very much was chosen. Next, letters of the alphabet were taught, and they were related to certain words in the song that he would sing. Then he learned the parts of the song which were sung in concert, and this led into reading the rest of the words in the song. Once he had acquired enough reading skill and personal confidence, the transition to regular reading materials was a relatively easy process.

Comment. The following points are of interest.

1. A shift occurred from rewards that were entertaining to rewards that were entertaining as well as educational in nature.
2. A gradual approach was used to the introduction of reading materials.
3. The reward was given after he worked on his reading assignment.
4. George's interest in piano was used as a source of reward.

Problem: General misbehavior

Reward: Social recognition and choice of other rewards

One principal, concerned about the amount of misbehavior in his building, instituted a rule that misbehaving students should be sent to the office only when they had had a good day. The class with the most names listed each week for outstanding behavior would then be given a choice of rewards—extended recess, dismissal at an earlier hour on Friday, a Friday afternoon movie, and the like. For that week, the outstanding class also received a plaque which was displayed in the showcase outside the principal's office. Management problems soon subsided.

Comment. This study makes clear the benefits that can occur from a focus on desirable behavior. It also points out a different role for school authority figures, such as the school principal. Also conspicuous was the provision for a choice of rewards.

•   •   •

Problem: Peers' reactions kept teacher from rewarding good academic
           work

Reward: Current expressions

, A senior high school teacher found that many students were ridiculed by their peers when she wrote on their papers complimentary phrases such as, "Nice job," "Thorough work," "Well thought out," and the like. Disconcerted by such peer reactions, she switched her choice of salutory remarks to comments such as "groovy," "fantastic," "out of this world," "Kapow," "Zowey," "Man, you must have been on a trip." Students soon reacted in a more favorable manner when she used novel rewards that they could "dig." In fact, they soon thought of other unusual expressions that she might use.

Comment. Instead of trying to fight a powerful peer group, this teacher wisely used the power of group dynamics to her advantage. Through the creative use of unusual rewards and through her use of contemporary expressions, she also offered the students a model who was human enough to have a sense of humor. The students could identify with this kind of teacher.

•   •   •

Problem: Hyperactive student

Reward: Walking in back of class

One teacher was visibly upset over the presence of an acting-out child in her kindergarten class. When queried about the student's appropriate behaviors, she insisted that he did nothing right. All he liked to do was wander around the back of the room and browse at the things back there. Following a conversation with the school psychologist, "remaining in his seat" was selected as a target behavior and browsing in the back of the room was to be the reward. A timer was set and would ring softly after he spent five minutes in his seat. He then was told to browse in the back of the room. After three minutes, the bell rang again, and he was told to take his seat. Gradually, the in-seat time (a low-frequency activity) required to earn the "travel time" (a high-frequency activity) was increased. Initially, Tom only had to sit in the seat, but gradually he had to complete short assignments in order to browse. By using this procedure, Tom became responsive to the teacher's request and his wandering ceased. Under this regimen, Tom was not defying the teacher's authority when he was out of his seat. He was doing only what his teacher allowed him to do. Furthermore, given this arrangement, the teacher no longer rewarded Tom's misbehavior by paying attention to him, for example, "Get back in your seat."

Comment. The following points are of special interest: (1) The teacher selected a specific target behavior to modify. (2) The teacher used an enjoyable activity (walking in back of room) on a contingent basis to increase the frequency of a nonenjoyable activity (staying in seat). (3) Tom was gradually weaned from "travel time" as a reward as in-seat activities became more satisfying. (4) The school mental health specialist served in a consultative capacity to the teacher.

·   ·   ·

Problem: Rowdy behavior in study hall
Reward: An activity

One beginning teacher used the novel reward of killing flies to maintain quiet in a normally rowdy study hall composed of 36 students (29 boys and 16 of them on the ninth grade football team!). The use of fly killing was a natural reward, since the room was infested with flies and a solution was needed. The entire football squad armed with books, magazines, and construction paper came up with an answer. After stopping the confusion, the teacher announced that the students who studied and were quiet during the hour would have the last five minutes free to participate in the war on the flies or to remain seated as rooting spectators. This novel reward worked effectively as the students learned to come into the room, sit down, and open their books, waiting and watching the clock until fly-killing time arrived.

When the fly population dropped off, the students continued the desirable study hall behavior for "a free time" period the last five minutes of each study hall session.

Comment. Who would have ever thought of fly killing as an activity reward to be earned for acceptable behavior? The answer is, of course, an observant teacher with practical ingenuity. Again we observe that behavior modification techniques can be applied to the class as a whole.

·   ·   ·

Problem: Carving up desk
Reward: Appropriate carving tasks when lessons were completed

Jim, a fourth grader, would much rather carve desks than do his assignments. His carvings were never random but involved a definite design —a complete circle with tiny circles surrounding it. His carving tools consisted of pens, pencils, rulers, and compasses. Year after year, Jim produced a new masterpiece. Finally, the teacher decided to capitalize on Jim's interest and talent by purchasing an inexpensive carving set. This was to be used only when Jim had completed his assigned work. Before the teacher presented the carving set to Jim, she first interested him in Indian history and the type of carvings they made by exposing him to different designs and patterns.

By the end of the school year, Jim was working more consistently, and instead of his usual desk masterpiece he produced a wall covering that was displayed in the year-end school art show.

Comment. In this instance, the teacher was able to turn the student's vice into virtue. Where this is not possible, for example, throwing paint on the walls, some form of restitution (punishment) is warranted as a means of coping with vandalism.

•   •   •

Problem: Teaching a deprived adolescent to read
Reward: Money

A fascinating investigation of remedial reading by Staats and Butterfield (1965) combined the use of two emerging approaches to the mental health problems of children, namely, behavior modification principles and the use of nonprofessionals. The subject for this study was a 14-year-old culturally deprived juvenile delinquent who had a long history of delinquency and maladjustment. His difficulties in school, in part, were attributable to his lack of academic skills and to his failure to respond to traditional classroom reinforcers. He had a full-scale IQ of 90 on the Weschler Intelligence Scale for children. His Verbal Scale IQ was 77, however, which would indicate a slow rate of school learning ability. The method of treatment relied on an extrinsic token reinforcement system with three types of tokens being used. A blue token was worth one tenth of one cent. A white token was worth one third of one cent. And a red token was worth one half of one cent. The tokens could be used to purchase a variety of items. That is, the child could choose his own reward. Materials from the Science Research Associates reading kits were adapted for use in the study. Vocabulary words were typed on separate three by five inch cards. Oral reading materials of paragraph length also were typed on separate five by eight inch cards so that each story could be presented. Comprehension questions were typed on eight and one-half by thirteen inch paper, and they were used to promote the understanding of silent reading materials. The objective was to develop remedial reading procedures that could be applied in a standard manner so as to permit the use of nonprofessionals who were trained in this procedure. The tutor in the study was a probation officer. Correct responses on the first trial yielded a token of high value, whereas correct responses that were made following errors yielded tokens of lower reinforcement value. Forty hours of remedial reading spread over a four and one-half month interval yielded considerable success. For example, the boy's reading ability rose from a beginning second grade level to a fourth grade level. This gain might not seem impressive except for the fact that this boy accomplished more in reading during this four and one-half month interval than he did in all of his previous eight and one-half years of schooling. Moreover, he passed all of his courses in school for the first time, his misbehavior became less frequent, and his general attitude toward school improved. Other points of interest include the fact that the subject received only $20.31 worth of tokens and that reading itself became reinforcing, so that more reading responses were made per reinforcer as time went on. The most important educational implication stemming from this case study is that standard reading materials can be adapted for relatively uniform type of presentations by training subprofessionals in the context of reinforcement principles. Later research (Staats et al., 1967) based on mentally retarded, culturally disadvantaged, and emotionally disturbed junior high school age subjects provided a more general test of these procedures and, by and large, confirmed their practical value. High school students and adult volunteers served as the tutors in this later research project.

.   .   .

Problem: Increasing academic performance in hard-core delinquents
Reward: Points to be exchanged for money

Another impressive illustration of the behavior modification approach has been carried out at the National Training School for Boys by Cohen et al. (1966). This project has been entitled CASE (Contingencies Applicable for Special Education). The specific target behavior in this study—academic performance—was shaped through the use of programmed instruction. Once a student successfully completed 90 percent of a unit, he was eligible to take an examination on which he could earn points worth one cent each. These points then could be spent for cokes, potato chips, items from Sears Roebuck, entrance into the lounge to visit with friends, book rentals, time in the library, and the like. Cohen and his associates reported that the systematic contingent application of reinforcement yielded best results when it took place in a highly structured environment that increased the likelihood of prosocial behaviors and decreased the likelihood of antisocial behaviors. To this end, a special environment was prepared which consisted of classrooms, study booths, control rooms, a library, a store, and a lounge. The results reflected a gradual shifting away from material reinforcers, for example, cokes, toward more educationally relevant rewards, for example, new programs. Aside from the enormous surge in educational activities, there were also favorable changes in the social behavior of the subjects. In fact, there were no discipline problems or property destruction in a four and one-half month period.

Note. The findings of these last two studies have considerable significance in the light of the shortage of mental health specialists and remedial teachers. The writer knows of no school district that has a sufficient number of remedial reading specialists or, for that matter, the enabling funds to employ them in the needed quantities. The tendency for gains to spread beyond the cognitive and academic areas into the social and emotional realms also merits close attention, since it applies to one role that the school can legitimately and apparently successfully assume relative to mental health. Remedial programs of this nature offer students a reality-based therapy that is not typically achieved in the insulated "talk-therapy" sessions in the clinician's office. These two studies also highlight the need to gear rewards to the student's developmental level.

The above study was carried out in the confines of a residential setting. How might these techniques be modified for use with antisocial students in a public school setting?

• • •

Problem: Underachievement in reading

Reward: Riddles and rhymes

Mike was a bright, eight-year-old boy whose reading skills were deficient with respect to both his grade level and his mental maturity. His lack of confidence in his own reading ability was readily apparent. His resistance was sometimes expressed openly, for example, "How much more of this stuff do I have to do?," "I'll read one more paragraph and that's all." On other occasions his resistance was more passive in nature and took the form of foot dragging.

In an effort to increase Mike's motivation, an educational contract was set up. If Mike concentrated on his reading for 15 minutes, he could select an activity that he enjoyed from a reinforcement menu. Mike had a fascination for riddles and rhymes, as he liked to use them to stump his better reading friends. Accordingly, he selected them as his reward.

Here are some samples:

> One for the cut worm,
> Two for the crow,
> Three for the chickens,
> And four to grow.

> I had a little dog, his name was Tim:
> I put him in a bathtub to see if he could swim;
> He drank all the water and ate all the soap,
> And almost died with a bubble in his throat.

> He wears his hat upon his neck
> Because he has no head
> And he never takes his hat off
> Until you're sick in bed.
> (A medicine bottle)

Contingency contracting in conjunction with the use of reinforcement menus over the year resulted in a significant improvement in Mike's reading. These gains kept him from repeating third grade.

Comment. This case depicts the use of an academic activity as a reward. The fact that a poor reader would select this type of activity is, at first glance, somewhat unexpected and highlights the importance of providing a choice in the selection of rewards. Notice that the reward was given after the completion of the contingency contract.

·   ·   ·

Problem: Teaching reading to an autistic child
Reward: Gum drops, interest in jigsaw puzzles

The use of operant conditioning techniques is illustrated in this case study, which represents one of the few explicit attempts to teach reading to a thirteen-year-old autistic child who had not developed speech. Hewett (1964) noted the boy's interest in jigsaw puzzles, letters, and gumdrops and took advantage of these interests in setting up a simple operant conditioning model. The six stages used in this boy's educational programming were as follows.

1. The associating of picture cards with the concrete objects.

2. The matching of picture and word symbols.

3. The building of a 55-word sight vocabulary.

4. The classification of words and pictures.

(These four stages required most of the first year of the educational programming. By then the student was interested in learning, and the teacher had taken on secondary reinforcement value.)

5. At this point, he was taught the alphabet in order to promote his communication skills. The boy still did not talk.

6. Having mastered the alphabet, he was taught to write simple phrases and was held for these in making his needs known.

The author states that the acquisition of rudimentary reading and writing skills increased his interest in his surroundings and rendered him more susceptible to control.

Note. Given ordinary, instructional techniques, this youngster would have been considered unteachable—a backward case unfit for school in even a residential setting. Autistic youngsters also have acquired speech through the use of conditioning models (Hewett, 1965). The acquisition of reading skills and speech, although not constituting a cure for these severe disabilities, does afford a significant means for social interaction and reality contacts.

Problem: Promoting motivation among emotionally disturbed students
Rewards: Tangible through intellectual success

Another recent development that bears on such germane issues as classroom discipline, educational sequencing, and pupil motivation is Hewett's engineered classroom. Based on a behavior modification model, the engineered classroom is designed to implement his hierarchy of educational tasks, a hierarchy that takes into account the normal stages of psychoeducational development in which disturbed children are often deficient (Hewett, 1967). This theoretical framework for teacher-pupil interactions allows the teacher to adopt a developmental viewpoint and to set the realistic educational goals for emotionally disturbed children with learning disabilities.

Each of the seven levels in this hierarchy (see Table 2.10) is concerned with the reciprocal tasks of the students and the teacher in the development of a working educational relationship. Whereas the average child has successfully mastered the first five levels in this hierarchy prior to school entrance, this is not the case with the majority of emotionally disturbed pupils. As Hewett (1967) observes, many disturbed youngsters lack the readiness necessary for a successful school adjustment

TABLE 2.10

Description of the Hierarchy of Educational Tasks

Hierarchy Level	Attention	Response	Order	Exploratory	Social	Mastery	Achievement
Child's problem	Inattention due to withdrawal or resistance	Lack of involvement and unwillingness to respond in learning	Inability to follow directions	Incomplete or inaccurate knowledge of environment	Failure to value social approval or disapproval	Deficits in basic adaptive and school skills not in keeping with IQ	Lack of self motivation for learning
Educational task	Get child to pay attention to teacher and task	Get child to respond to tasks he likes and which offer promise of success	Get child to complete tasks with specific starting points and steps leading to a conclusion	Increase child's efficiency as an explorer and get him involved in multisensory exploration of his environment	Get child to work for teacher and peer group approval and to avoid their disapproval	Remediation of basic skill deficiencies	Development of interest in acquiring knowledge
Learner reward	Provided by tangible rewards (e.g., food, money, tokens)	Provided by gaining social attention	Provided through task completion	Provided by sensory stimulation	Provided by social approval	Provided through task accuracy	Provided through intellectual task success
Teacher structure	Minimal	Still limited	Emphasized	Emphasized	Based on standards of social appropriateness	Based on curriculum assignments	Minimal

Source. "Educational Engineering with Emotionally Disturbed Children," by Frank Hewett, *Exceptional Children*, Vol. 33, 1967.

because they have difficulty paying attention, following directions, getting along with others and the like. Hewett does more than simply enumerate the levels in the education hierarchy through which disturbed pupils should progress. He goes on to describe the educational tasks, the types of rewards, and the degrees of teacher structure that correspond to the level at which the child is currently functioning.

Perhaps, the main merit of Hewett's hierarchy is that it allows the teacher to assess the child's specific liabilities and to establish an educational program for a particular child on the basis of this assessment. For example, with a child at a primitive level of development, it would be necessary for the teacher to secure the child's attention through the use of concrete rewards before advancing to the second level where the basic concern is getting the child involved in learning. Or, for an unruly pupil, it may be necessary to focus on a social level in which social appropriateness is basic before advancing to the mastery or achievement levels.

Notice that the nature of the rewards varies with the developmental readiness of the child. The diversity of rewards (concrete, social attention, task completion, sensory stimulation, task accuracy, and task success) used in this approach takes into consideration the complexity of human motivation and learning. It is certainly more than a narrowly conceived behavior modification paradigm based on M and Ms as the primary reinforcement. Notice, also, that the degree of teacher structure varies with the developmental level of the child. In keeping with this learning theory approach, the child is assisted along the educational hierarchy by completing small steps at a time. Hence, instead of unrealistically demanding that the disturbed pupil perform the ultimate in desired classroom behavior, namely, the mastery level characterized by self-motivation and successful achievement, the teacher guides the pupil toward that goal through a series of successive approximations. That is, the child achieves some degree of mastery at one level before proceeding to the next level, until he ultimately reaches the mastery level.

In implementing his hierarchical approach to the education of disturbed children, Hewett advocates that the physical environment of the classroom be divided into three sections which parallel levels in the hierarchy (see Figure 2.1). Thus, there is a mastery achievement center, where academic lessons are undertaken, an exploratory social center that is further subdivided into a science, art, and communications area and, finally, an order center in which skills at the first three levels of the hierarchy are developed. Check marks are also given to the students in accordance with very specific standards. Thus, for example, two check marks are given for starting an assignment, a task that falls at the attention level of the hierarchy, and three are given for completing the assign-

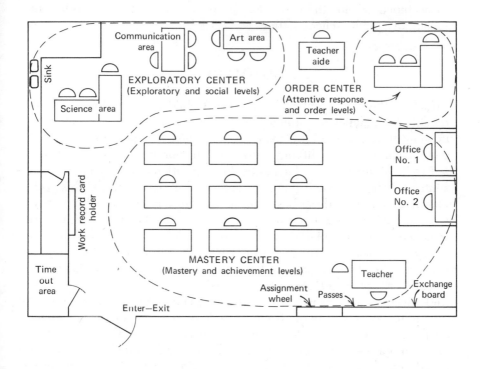

FIGURE 2.1

The floorplan of an engineered classroom. (From "Educational Engineering with Emotionally Disturbed Children," by Frank Hewett, *Exceptional Children*, Vol. 33, 1967.)

ment, a task that falls at the response level. When maladaptive behaviors occur, for example, daydreaming, assignments are quickly altered. Although Hewett does provide a list of student interventions that correspond to the levels of the hierarchy, the teacher is allowed considerable latitude in the choice of intervention techniques when undesirable behavior occurs. A child, for instance, who has become bored and restless at the mastery level might be given a pass to the exploratory center where he can engage in an art, science, or communication activity. The teacher thereby offers the student an opportunity for motoric release of his tensions while minimizing the need for disciplinary action. Furthermore, the pupil learns that certain types of behaviors are appropriate and specific to each of the designated areas of the classroom. Hewett believes that given a well-organized classroom, an aide to assist the teacher, and the use of concrete rewards on occasion, that this design can be functional for the education of disturbed children in both institutional and public school settings.

SUMMARY

Much of the excitement of learning that children bring to school can probably be maintained through the careful use of rewards. Positive reinforcement is regarded by many psychologists as, perhaps, the most potent technique for modifying voluntary behavior. Positive reinforcement has two basic functions—it facilitates the acquisition of new behaviors and maintains behaviors once they are acquired. Teachers using this technique must consider these basic questions: How often should a reward be given? When should rewards be given? And what types of reward should be given? Regular rewards help a student to "catch on" to new behavior, whereas occasional rewards help the student to "hold on" to behaviors already learned. To be considered reasonably socialized, a student must eventually become responsive to occasional rewards, delayed rewards, and social-verbal rewards. The transition from regular rewards to occasional ones, from immediate rewards to delayed ones, and from a strictly tangible reward to intrinsic or social ones must be gradual in nature, however. In many instances, it is initially necessary to reward approximations of the desired behavior. The use of a reinforcement menu is one of the best ways for determining what is rewarding for a student at a given point in time. When the use of positive reinforcement fails, it is often because the teacher has set his criterion or standard too high, for example, permitting absolutely no talking during study hour, or because the rewards offered for desirable behavior are not as appealing as the ones stemming from misbehavior. In such instances, it is necessary to take smaller steps and/or to provide more attractive payoffs.

Rules can play an important role in classroom management provided that they are definable, reasonable, and enforceable. It is generally a good idea to involve students in the establishment and enforcement of rules. It is also desirable to relax the rules and to have an enjoyable time with the students once the work period is over. Not only does peer group influence constitute a persuasive force but opportunities for self-management and the discussion of rules is essential to promoting internalized controls. Educational contracts also constitute an effective vehicle for enhancing the academic and personal adjustment of students. Remember that the "poorly motivated" student is one who engages in behaviors that he finds more rewarding than the ones in which the teacher wants him to engage.

REFERENCES

Addison, R. M., and Homme, L. E. The reinforcing event (RE) menu. *National Society for Programmed Instruction Journal,* 1966, **5** (1), 8–9.

Cohen, H. L. Educational therapy: The design of learning environments. In J. M. Shlien (ed.), *Research in Psychotherapy.* Washington, D.C.: American Psychological Association, 1968, pp. 21–53.

Glasser, W. *Mental Health or Mental Illness?* New York: Harper & Brothers, 1961.

Hall, V. R., Lund, D., and Jackson, D. Effects of teacher attention on study behavior. *Journal of Applied Behavior Analysis,* 1968, **1,** 1–12.

Hartup, W. Friendship status and the effectiveness of peers as reinforcing agents. *J. Exp. Child. Psychol.,* 1964, **1,** 154–162.

Hewett, F. Teaching reading to an autistic boy through operant conditioning. *The Reading Teacher,* 1964, **17,** 613–618.

Hewett, F. Teaching speech to an autistic child through operant conditioning. *American Journal of Orthopsychiatry,* 1965, **35,** 927–936.

Hewett, F. Educational engineering with emotionally disturbed children. *Except. Child.,* 1967, **33,** 459–467.

Homme, L. E. *How to use contingency contracting in the classroom.* Urbana: Research Press, 1969.

Hunter, M. *Reinforcement.* El Segundo, California: TIP Publications, 1967.

Levin, G., and Simmons, J. Response to praise by emotionally disturbed boys. *Psychological Reports,* 1962, **2,** 10. (a)

Levin, G., and Simmons, J. Response to food and praise by emotionally disturbed boys. *Psychological Reports,* 1962, **2,** 539–546. (b)

Madsen, C. H., Becker, W., and Thomas, D. R. Rules, Praise and Ignoring: Elements of elementary classroom control. *Journal of Applied Behavior Analysis,* 1968, **1,** 139–150.

Madsen, C. H., Becker, W. C., Thomas, D. R., Koser, L., and Plager, E. An analysis of the reinforcing function of "sit-down" commands in R. K. Parker (ed.). *Readings in Educational Psychology,* Boston: Allyn & Bacon, Inc., 1968, 265–278.

Neisworth, J., Deno, S., and Jenkins, J. *Student Motivation and Classroom Management—a behavioristic approach.* Newark, Delaware: Behavior Technics, Inc., 1969.

Patterson, J., and Anderson, D. Peers as social reinforcers. *Child Develpm.,* 1964, **35,** 951–960.

Smith, J.M., and Smith, D. *Child Management: A program for Parents.* Ann Arbor: Ann Arbor Publishers, 1966.

Staats, A. W., and Butterfield, W. H. Treatment of nonreading in a culturally deprived juvenile delinquent: An application of reinforcement principles. *Child Develpm.,* 1965, **36,** 925–942.

Staats, A. W., Minke, K. A., Goodwin, W., and Landeen, J. Cognitive behavior modification: "motivated learning" reading treatment with subprofessional therapy-technicians. *Behavior Research and Therapy*, 1967, **5**, 283–299.

Stiavelli, R. S., and Shirley, D. T. The citizens' council: A technique for managing behavior disorders in the educationally handicapped class. *Journal for School Psychology*, **6**, 1968, 147–153.

Titkin, S., and Hartup, W. Sociometric status and the reinforcing effectiveness of children's peers. *J. Exp. Child Psychol.*, 1965, **2**, 306–315.

3

Modeling and Observational Learning

According to Bandura, who is the primary exponent of behavior change through modeling and observational learning, positive reinforcement is an exceedingly inefficient and tedious method for promoting the acquisition of *new* adaptive learnings. Effective as positive rewards are for the strengthening of already existent behaviors, they often demand ingenious and time-consuming manipulations to produce new response patterns that can then be rewarded. As we pointed out earlier, the new behavior, or some approximation thereof, must first occur before appropriate rewards can be applied. Techniques that involve positive reward have not always proved economical when the acquisition of complex behavior is sought. Moreover, trial-and-error learning can prove hazardous in many natural settings. For example, if we waited for individuals who are learning to swim to exhibit spontaneously a proper stroke or an approximation thereof and then rewarded them, few of them would live long enough to become adept swimmers.[1] As Bandura (1969) points out, "It would be difficult to imagine a culture in which the language, mores, vocational and avocational patterns, familial customs, and educational, social and political practices were shaped in each new member through a gradual

[1] Reward procedures can be used alone to evoke new patterns of behavior when (1) the individual already has the readily available component skills, (2) the environmental conditions exist that are capable of arousing actions that are similar to the desired behaviors, and (3) the student and teacher possess sufficient endurance to employ such time-consuming methods (Bandura, 1969).

process of differential reinforcement without the response guidance of models who exemplify the accumulated cultural repertories in their own behavior." Under most natural learning conditions, social behaviors are typically learned through modeling in large segments or in toto instead of being acquired in a piecemeal, trial-and-error manner. The sheer simplicity of modeling procedures, Bandura argues, justifies their use in preference to or in combination with positive reinforcement techniques. There is no question but that modeling procedures are an economical means of transmitting new responses, especially when a combination of verbalizing models and demonstrations are used. In actual classroom situations these two behavior formation techniques—positive reinforcement and modeling—are typically combined with the student obtaining a reward when he imitates an act performed by the model. Once acquired, the behavior can often be maintained without external reinforcement, since human beings learn to reinforce themselves for behaving in certain ways. Bandura, himself stresses the point that the combination of modeling and reinforcement procedures is probably the most effective method of "transmitting, eliciting, and maintaining social response patterns."

Teachers, who are aware of the importance of observational learning, realize that we often teach by example. Since the learning and regulation of both intellectual and social skills can be strongly influenced through examples of socially acceptable behavior, teachers are often able to influence the behavior of their students through the use of modeling. Although much remains to be learned about modeling procedures, these techniques are, as we shall learn, well suited for use by educational personnel with withdrawn students, antisocial youngsters, and those who simply are deficient with respect to adequate social and scholastic skills.

Unfortunately, despite its having a distinct utilitarian value, this technique has been neglected in the management and modification of deviant behavior. Training institutions have long recognized the importance of modeling procedures in the preparation of future teachers and, therefore, have attempted to provide adequate models in the form of critic teachers; however, training institutions have devoted less attention to the use of modeling procedures as a means of influencing the behavior of the pupils with whom the teachers will have to work.

EXPOSURE TO MODELS

Exposure to models can be accomplished in a variety of ways. To date, the live model has been mostly commonly employed, with teachers generally demonstrating certain behaviors that they want their students to inculcate. But, as we shall learn, the use of peers as live models can also prove extremely effective, especially at the high school level when social acceptance and approval (social reinforcers) are as much, or more, in the peer group leader's hands as in the teachers'. The use of real live models entails, however, both advantages and disadvantages (Krumboltz and Thoresen, 1969). On the positive side, the greater vividness may prove highly motivating and arousing, thereby facilitating the modeling process. Live models have proved instrumental in teaching delinquents how to act during a job interview, how to react in conversations with policemen, and how to resist undesirable peer influence that would lead to disruptive classroom behavior (Sarason and Ganzer, 1969). They have also been used to good advantage in teaching schizophrenic children how to play and to interact verbally, thus reducing the social isolation and withdrawal typical of this condition (Lovaas et al., 1967). On the other hand, it is sometimes more difficult to control the behavior of a live model. That is, live models do not always perform in the precise ways that we might want. Teachers, for example, do not always behave in a way consistent with their preachings, and the peer group does not always demonstrate the kinds of behavior that we deem appropriate or relevant to our objectives. Furthermore, the real life modeling experience might prove too overwhelming for the student. Symbolic models (video-taped models, film strip, written stories or scripts, and audio tapes) by contrast provide greater control in terms of timing, format, and content (Krumboltz and Thoresen, 1969). Examples relating to the classroom usage of both live and symbolic models are provided in the latter part of the chapter.

BASIC EFFECTS OF MODELING

The Acquisition of New Behaviors

Simple reflection and observation indicate that much of our behavior is learned through imitation rather than through direct instruction. Indeed, practically all learnings can be acquired on a vicarious basis through the observation of other people's behavior and its consequences for them. Students can acquire complex intellectual and social competencies merely by observing the performance of suitable models. Speech, foreign languages, vocational skills, hobbies, specialized technical skills, athletics, dancing, love making, and the art of social conversation can all be learned through this technique.

Emotional reactions can also be conditioned simply by witnessing the affective responses of others who are undergoing pleasurable or painful experiences. Approach and avoidance behaviors can be learned in this way. Barnwell and Sechrest (1965), for example, found that both first and third grade students selected a task on which they observed their classmates receiving praise and avoided a task on which they witnessed other children receiving disapproval. Likewise, avoidant behaviors such as a fear of the teacher can be established simply by a student's observing his classmates being scolded. Similarly, approach responses to a teacher can be established by watching one's classmates having pleasant inter- actions with him. Aggressive behaviors can also be learned through ex- posure to aggressive models. Conversely, it is possible to teach hyperaggressive and domineering children new ways of handling frus- trating situations. One investigator (Chittenden, 1942) had a group of acting-out children observe and discuss a series of eleven 15-minute plays in which dolls, representing preschool children, exhibited an aggressive and a cooperative solution to the childhood quarrels that were similar to the ones that they were likely to encounter in their daily associations. The consequences of aggression were shown to be unpleasant and those of cooperativeness to be rewarding. Two boys fighting over a wagon, for example, were both depicted as unhappy because they broke the wagon during their struggle. By contrast, the two boys who took turns with the wagon wound up feeling happy and enjoying themselves. Acting-out children who viewed these two different reactions and consequences showed a decrease in dominative aggressiveness. Of even greater interest is the finding that these changes in behavior carried over to the actual nursery school and were still evident on follow-up a month later. Another investigator has shown the effectiveness of similar procedures with older children (Gillelman, 1965). In brief, the point to be underscored is that many varieties of emotional responsiveness can be learned on a vicarious basis.

One type of learning having widespread significance that deserves special comment pertains to the development of a favorable attitude in students toward the subject matter that they are studying. As Mager (1968) points out, learning is for future use, and the likelihood of the student's putting his knowledges and skills to use is influenced by his attitudes toward them. Things that are disliked tend to be forgotten. Things that are enjoyed tend to be remembered. And, of course, teachers do influence attitudes not only toward a given subject matter but toward learning itself. Many students come to school with varying attitudes toward learning and specific subjects. Some of these attitudes are negative in nature, some positive, and perhaps many neutral in that they might not know much about given topics. In any event, one essential objective for teachers is to develop and/or to maintain a favorable attitude toward learning. For if a student is favorably inclined toward a given subject, he keeps coming back for more of it, he seeks out new experiences with it, and the more hurdles he will overcome to come into contact with it and to stay in contact with it. In short, he develops approach tendencies toward the subject matter and, to some degree, toward learning in general. By contrast, if he develops negative attitudes, he is apt to develop avoidance tendencies. To a great extent, students' attitudes are based on the *conditions* surrounding a subject and on the *consequences* of coming into contact with the subject. As was noted in the discussion of positive reinforcement, when actions lead to desirable consequences and are associated with pleasant conditions, they are likely to occur again. This does not mean that instructional situations should just be fun and that hard work is not required. What it does mean is that, given appropriate conditions, students will want to work longer and harder. As a result, they become more self-directing, which is precisely the object of our disciplinary practices. In addition to conditions and consequences, modeling can be effectively used to promote a love for learning. As Mager (1968) states, "if we would maximize subject matter approach tendencies in our students, we must exhibit those behaviors ourselves." That is, we must act in a way that we want our students to act. Just as we cannot teach students courtesy by shouting and screaming at them or teach students democracy by not giving them a voice in classroom discipline, so we cannot foster enthusiasm about any given topic through a display of apathy and indifference. Although a display of interest and excitement does not constitute a surefire guarantee that our students will display similar feelings, it does increase the probabilities appreciably. We now have research evidence supporting the common sense notion that teaching is less effective if you teach one thing and model something else, than if you practice what you teach (Rosenhan et al., 1968).

Inhibition and Disinhibition

Imitation not only promotes the learning of new behaviors but also can strengthen or weaken the inhibition of previously learned responses. In this section, we discuss the effects of vicarious learning on behaviors that are already a part of us. Generally, we become more inhibited when we observe others experience negative consequences for engaging in behavior similar to ours. In other words, vicarious punishment can produce suppressive effects. In fact, Benton (1967) found that vicarious punishment (that is, simply watching others being punished) results in the same amount of inhibition as directly experienced punishment.

By contrast, we tend to be less inhibited when we witness others being rewarded for engaging in behavior similar to ours. That is, positive reinforcement also can be experienced on a vicarious basis with the result that we become increasingly open in the expression of given behaviors. Individuals who see others being rewarded for aggressive acts (for example, getting their own way as a result of threatening others) become increasingly inclined to act out their own aggressive feelings. It is interesting to note that an observer's misbehavior increases when he witnesses a model misbehave but not experience the punishment usually associated with it. These findings suggest that a teacher's failure to react to formerly prohibited activities actually, through contrast, may constitute a sense of positive vicarious reinforcement for the misbehaving student (Walters and Parke, 1965). This result is fine if the teacher wants to increase a given behavior. It may not be so good, however, if this is a behavior in need of suppression.

Some of the most fascinating and relevant work regarding the classroom use of vicariously experienced rewards and punishments has been done by Kounin (1970) on what is called the "ripple effect"—a concept which refers to the fact that the transactions between the teacher and wayward students have an impact on the other students who view the incidents.[2] Several factors appear to influence the nature and the extent of the ripple effect, or emotional contagion. First, teacher firmness is important, since it not only reduces the deviancy of the offender but that of the witnesses. The teacher who can adapt a "no nonsense," "I mean what I say" approach is in a good position to enforce compliance with the rules. The ripple effect works in the teacher's favor when he follows through or enforces the rules, that is, when other students observe that the offender is punished. However, when other students see that the troublemaker gets away with his misbehavior, the ripple effect then will work to the teacher's disadvantage. If the teacher tells a student to go to the office and he tells the teacher "Go to hell" and has a cigarette in the lavatory, the probabilities are high that the teacher's difficulties will be compounded. As is evident by now, the consequences arising from one's misbehavior has a significant impact on the audience. In general, witnesses to submissive or compliant offenders rated their teachers as "more capable of handling kids" than witnesses to offenders who successfully defied teacher authority. Furthermore, more learning occurred in groups in which the offenders complied with teacher reprimands than in groups where the offenders resisted teacher reprimands.

Although firmness and follow-through are essential, the teacher should avoid being rough and harsh, since these qualities not only tended to

---

[2] Extinction and desensitization procedures, which are discussed in later chapters also can be used on a vicarious basis.

increase disruptive behavior among the witnesses but to lower students' estimations of the teacher's helpfulness, likeability, and fairness. Roughness is not just an increased degree of firmness. And it is undesirable because it decreases the likelihood that the student will model his behavior after the teacher's. That is, it interferes with identificatory learnings.

The deviant's prestige also plays a critical role in the ripple effect. In general, the ripple effect is greater when high-status troublemakers are involved than when low-status deviants are involved. When the teacher successfully manages the high-prestige deviant, the ripple effect works to an even greater degree in his favor. However, when the high-prestige deviant gets his way, then the ripple effect works to an even greater extent to the teacher's disadvantage. Regardless of outcome, the ripple effect is greater when high-status deviants are involved. Since what happens to the leaders is very important, teachers would do well to discover what control techniques cause high-status deviants to respond in a compliant manner (Gnagey, 1968). The teacher who controls and dispenses reinforcers (pleasant or unpleasant) that are capable of influencing the peer group leader's behavior has at his disposal a potent means for changing the behavior of the entire class. This point is stressed by Bandura (1969) who points out that "The attitudes and actions of entire groups can be modified most rapidly and pervasively by changing the conduct norms modeled by key sources of behavioral contagion, whereas attempts to alter the behavior of each member, individually would prove exceedingly laborious and ineffectual."

The impact of the ripple effect also depends on the *focus* of the teacher's discipline. In disciplining a student, a teacher can focus on the achievement to be accomplished (a task-focus) or on the relationship that exists between himself and the student (an approval-focus). Consider the student who talks during math study time. The teacher who used task-focused techniques might say something like, "George, you will have to be quiet or you won't get your math assignment done," whereas a teacher who uses approval-focused techniques might say in a disappointed tone, "Jim, I didn't think you'd do something like that to me after I told you not to." Students who witnessed the use of task-focused techniques increased their estimates of the teacher's skill more than did witnesses to approval-focused methods. Moreover, subject matter interest increased among students who viewed task-focused techniques. This was not true for the students who viewed approval-focused methods.[3]

[3] It might well be that the typical teacher-pupil relationship is not personally in-

The ripple effect is also influenced by the characteristics of the audience. For example, there are differences with regard to the ripple effect between students with high achievement motivation and those who are less well motivated. As expected, highly motivated students regard deviancies as more serious, perceive the teacher's control techniques as more fair, and side with the teacher against the troublemakers. They also respond to witnessed disciplinary measures by paying closer attention to the task at hand and by behaving even better.

Bandura (1969) made a point of the fact that it is generally easier to disinhibit than to inhibit various patterns of adjustment through vicarious means. The basic reason for this is that inhibited behaviors are often personally rewarding to the student but are suppressed because of others' negative reactions. Therefore, the individual does not have to witness very *many* others successfully engaging in behaviors in which he would like to participate before he actually will do likewise. On the other hand, it is more difficult to inhibit adjustment patterns through vicarious punishment (or direct punishment, for that matter) because they commonly are immediately satisfying to the student. Accordingly, teachers should expect that students will require a more prolonged exposure to desirable models if undesirable behaviors are to be held in check.

Eliciting Effect

Thus far we have discussed the effects of modeling on (1) the acquisition of new behaviors, and (2) the weakening or strengthening of inhibitory responses already existing in the observer. But modeling has yet another effect—the eliciting effect. It differs from the two effects discussed earlier in that the imitated behavior is neither new nor has it been previously punished. In other words, the eliciting effect refers to the triggering of previously learned behaviors that are neutral or socially sanctioned. In this type of modeling effect, observation of the teacher's or peer's behavior provides discriminative cues that elicit ingrained responses of a similar and socially acceptable nature. The right word or cue from the teacher, for example, might facilitate behaviors such as volunteering to clean up the blackboards or woodshop, helping fellow students who are having trouble with an assignment, settling down to finish an assignment, or getting students to follow the example of a prestigeful peer.

tense enough to permit "withdrawal of love techniques" (personal disapproval) to be effective. One cannot threaten to take away a close relationship where none exists.

FACTORS INFLUENCING MODELING

Sheer exposure to a model is obviously no guarantee that the student will imitate what the teacher wants him to. Susceptibility to social modeling influence is largely determined by three factors—the characteristics of the model, the characteristics of the observer, and the consequences (positive and negative) that are associated with modeling behavior. The first set of factors relating to characteristics of the model include such things as:

a. The extent to which the teacher is perceived as possessing a high degree of competence, status, and control over resources.

b. The extent to which the teacher has been perceived as nurturant and supportive in the past.

c. The most contagious models are apt to be those who are major sources of support and control in his surroundings, namely, his parents, playmates and older children, and adults who play a prominent role in his everyday life.

d. The degree to which the student perceives the model as similar to himself.

e. The use of several models exhibiting similar behavior is more effective in changing behavior than the use of a single model.

f. The extent to which the model's behavior is a salient feature in the actions of a group to which the child already belongs or aspires to be a member (Bronfenbrenner, 1970).

Thus, for example, students readily identify with a nurturant teacher, school celebrities, and with older students. Characteristics of the observer that influence imitative behavior include factors such as: (a) the student's sex; (b) race; (c) socioeconomic level; and (d) personality characteristics (dependency needs, achievement motivation, hostility level, cooperativeness, and the like). Thus, we find that boys imitate aggressive behavior more readily than girls, dependent youngsters and those with a cooperative set (as opposed to a competitive set) are more susceptible to imitative influences, and that angry and authoritarian students respond readily to aggressive models (Flanders, 1968).

Outcomes of the modeled behavior are extremely important in determining the extent of imitation. In fact, the use of appealing incentives, in the majority of instances, can override the effects of model attributes and observer characteristics (Bandura, 1969). For example, a teacher having only average social power and status in the eyes of his students can still promote imitative behavior simply by telling them that they later will be asked to reproduce what he teaches them (that is, to model his behavior) and that they will be handsomely rewarded for so doing. In brief, the student will perform more of what he has learned if he has seen someone being reinforced for that performance, that is, if incentive conditions are right. On the other hand, as indicated previously, the student will not be as likely to engage in the kind of behavior for which he has seen others being punished.

The above findings, as Bronfenbrenner (1970) notes, stress the need for the teacher not only to serve as a motivating model but to actively "seek out, organize, develop, and coordinate the activities of other appropriate models and reinforcing agents both within the classroom and outside." Implementation of these findings argue for innovations in classroom structure such as teams, cooperative group competition, and organized patterns of mutual help (for example, assigning an older student of the same sex to work with a younger companion). Again we see the constructive potential inherent in the peer group in developing academic competence as well as social responsibility and consideration for others.

EXAMPLES OF MODELING

Problem: Developing interest in English literature

Technique: Use of teacher and peers as live models

Reading for many junior and senior high school students is a dull and sometimes painful activity. They fail to perceive its value as a learning tool and as a fascinating entertainment for leisure-time pursuits. In the light of the hostility and apathy among students in a required course, it is by no means an easy task for English teachers to instill an appreciation of literature.

One teacher, in response to this challenge, made it a practice to read a book of an entertaining and wholesome nature as the students filtered in for class. Sometimes, he would chuckle out loud, frown intensely, smile delightfully, or look deep in thought as a means of conveying interest in the book at hand. A student would always ask about the book or make a comment, for example "It must be funny to make you laugh." The teacher would reinforce the student's inquiry by telling the class the general plot of the story but not the outcome. In response to questions about how the story came out, he would say in an enthusiastic manner that he had not gotten that far yet. Occasionally, he would read some of the more humorous or exciting passages. He gave them just enough to whet their appetites. He would also seize this opportunity to ask how many other students had read interesting books lately. For example, knowing full well that George had read and thoroughly enjoyed a book about automobile racing, he might say, "George, weren't you reading a book about cars?" and thereby elicit a testimonial of sorts. The teacher would also unobtrusively ask, "What was the name of that book again?"

Comment. One of the teacher's main objectives is to help the students' develop a favorable attitude toward the subject matter. If a teacher succeeds in developing good reading skills in his students but accomplishes this objective in such an unstimulating or punishing way that the student does not enjoy reading and, consequently, does not read outside of the school situation, then there is serious question as to whether this teacher has indeed fulfilled his role.

Numerous studies show that students enjoy teachers who are enthusiastic about the topic. Enthusiasm is contagious. We all can probably recall becoming excited about a course primarily because of a zealous teacher. Personal indifference can be transformed into eager and pleasurable participation.

Again, we have seen the use of rewarded models, that is, how much the teacher and George enjoyed themselves through reading. This basically is the same strategy employed in television advertisements, namely if one uses brand X hair cream like the man on the screen, then one can reap the same rewards that he does.

· · ·

Problem: Perfectionistic tendencies

Modeling: Use of teacher, peers and parents

Jim, a nine-year-old fourth grader, is a "model student." He is responsive to teacher demands and is extremely meticulous in carrying out assignments. His perfectionistic tendencies are readily evident. If he has a math assignment and correctly answers 18 of the 20 problems, he focuses on the two that he got wrong. If a theme does not turn out the way that he wants it, he tears it up in disgust. In short, Jim becomes very self-punitive when he feels that there are shortcomings in his performance.

After discussing Jim with the school psychologist, the teacher launched a multipronged attack on the problem. Foremost among the strategies used were the following: Jim's comment that his teacher never made mistakes and that he shouldn't either led her to believe that she had been providing Jim with a perfectionistic model to live up to. She realized that she had also been inadvertently rewarding Jim's perfectionistic tendencies by praising him when he got "100" and by withholding praise when his paper was less than perfect. She knew he could be a good student and she expected him to be just that. Now she had to change her tactics somewhat. She still wanted him to be a competent student, but he had to learn that the world does not fall apart because of human errors.

One of the first steps that she took was to stop rewarding his flawless performances and to begin rewarding him for just good performance, for example, she would write on his paper "Jim, that was a tough assignment and you did a good job on it." In brief, she tried to ignore "undesirable" behavior—namely, perfectionistic behavior, and to strengthen desirable behavior—namely, "good performances."

Another technique that she used was to discuss some of the historically well-known people, carefully pointing out their strong points but also noting that all of them had failed at something in their lives. It was noted, for instance, that even the brilliant Einstein admitted confirming only one in a thousand of his ideas. Later, she asked the students to think about an incident that in some ways might be comparable to the ones discussed earlier. Jim was a little bit shaken after hearing about how many people had had events in their lives that did not go as planned. Then the teacher pointed out how she had "goofed" in her first year of teaching but how the occurrence of these errors had actually made her a better teacher and person today.

Another technique involved playing "stump the teacher." This game was used as a reward on Fridays when the class had worked hard. Students were free to ask any question on any subject. Jim's teacher, though competent, could not, of course, answer all of the questions addressed to her. Jim and the rest of the class would laugh when she did not know the answer, and she would laugh with them, thereby showing that she could be less than perfect and yet self-accepting. The message implicit in these modeling incidents was that "I don't know everything but yet I am an adequate and worthwhile person both in my own eyes and the eyes of others."

The teacher also taught Jim the difference between "good mistakes" and "poor mistakes." The former entail the use of the correct process even though the execution of the process leaves something to be desired. Through this technique, Jim was able to become more accepting of certain types of mistakes. Once he had learned to be more accepting of good mistakes, he was encouraged to become more accepting of the poor mistakes too.

The parents were also well aware of the stress and strain associated with their son's perfectionistic ways and were eager to do whatever they could. In a conference with the parents, the teacher explained some of the strategies that she had used in school and encouraged them to carry these over to the home. The father, a journalist, could point out, for instance, that he had to rewrite almost every article he published despite his years of experience and training. Yet, he was still respected as a person of talent. Such experiences were to be related in a casual, nonobvious way so that Jim would not get the impression that others were just trying to make him feel good following a "failure" experience. By the end of the school year, Jim no longer tore up papers in disgust. Although he still set high standards for himself, he seemed more self-accepting and reported that he could live with himself more easily now.

Comment. This study illustrates the use of a variety of live models in overcoming the fear of a sense of failure. Modeling techniques showed him that he was not the only person who had shortcomings. He also learned that he could regard himself as a worthwhile person despite making consistent, trivial errors. Also carefully notice how the teacher, on a gradual basis, helped him to become more accepting—first, of "good mistakes" and, then, of "poor mistakes." Again we see the important role that school mental health specialists can fulfill by consulting with teachers. More will be said of this desensitizing technique in the next chapter.

• • •

Problem: Returning a dropout to school
Technique: Modeling, rewarding curriculum

Bob was a sixteen-year-old black student in the eighth grade who had considerable difficulty getting along with his peers and teachers. Much of his difficulty centered around his poor relationship with whites. Because of his violent acting-out behavior, he was excluded from school for the remainder of the fall semester.

The immediate problem was how to get Bob back in school. Among other strategies, the plan of action called for one of the school's popular black football players (Lee), who was an adequate student, to meet on his own time with Bob at the YMCA or at the school athletic plant after school. A room was also made available for the purposes of personal discussions and tutoring. Their discussions would evolve around themes such as the importance of staying in school ("Man, you can't go anywhere without an education"), the importance of self-control ("A guy can't afford to blow his cool—on the athletic field or in class"), respecting

authority ("the coach or teacher knows best even though you might not
think so at the time"), not being baited by others ("You can't let others
sucker you"), and getting along with others (teamwork concept).

At present, Bob is back in school, and the school personnel recognize
how difficult it will be to have him remain there. Current plans include
continued sessions with Lee, the incorporation of a coordinated work-
study program so as to make school more immediately relevant and rewarding, additional tutoring on the ideas and concepts related to his
school program and job, and group role-playing sessions with the school
counselor around many of the themes that Lee earlier discussed with
Bob. Although only time will tell as to the success of this total program,
Bob is back in school and his overt hostility has diminished somewhat.
Furthermore, he has told Lee that he plans "to stick it (school) out" for
awhile, at least.

Comment. The following points are noteworthy. (1) The use of a peer
who is prestigeful, of the same race, and older (but not too old to lack
creditability) is an excellent way to facilitate the modeling effect. (2)
Nonprofessionals who are viewed as "one of us" can sometimes accomplish more than can "outside" professionals. In instances of this nature,
a two step communication-change program—from professional to nonprofessional to the student—is indicated. Unfortunately, we have not made
the most effective use of natural leaders as models in modifying the behavior of their followers. (3) Behavior problems frequently stem, in part,
from asking students to undertake assignments that are not meaningful
to them and/or are not consistent with their current abilities. For large
segments of our school population, we must radically revise the school
curriculum if it is to be a rewarding and a truly educational experience
for them. Dealing with hard-core students is doubly difficult when we
must deal with hard-core professionals who will not adapt their educational offerings to their students' needs.

•   •   •

Problem: "Smarting Off" In Class
Modeling: Ripple effect

Mr. M., who taught a required United States history course, ordinarily
ignored sly or sarcastic comments from students because of their infrequent occurrence. Ignoring these comments seemed to work well with
most students; however, one fellow in the class, a popular member of the
football team, would make wisecracks at every opportunity during class

discussions. Realizing that he was being tested and that this "smarting-off" could easily be contagious, Mr. M. decided to take a firm stand with respect to this disturbing behavior. The next time discourteous remarks were made, Mr. M. acted without hesitation. "Bob, you will have to leave the room and go to the office." Bob's reaction and that of the entire class was one of surprise—"you can't possibly do this" to one of our heroes. Bob was readmitted to the class following a brief apology to his classmates and Mr. M. Bob was not the only one to learn a lesson. His classmates quickly realized that if Mr. M. dared to set limits for such a popular student as Bob, they certainly would not be immune to similar sanctions. The class respected Mr. M. for his display of strength and fairness in not overlooking the rule infraction of a student who was very popular with other students and teachers.

Comment. This incident shows how the correction of a prestigeful leader can become a vicarious learning experience for those who witness the punishment. The value of "firmness" and a "I mean what I say" approach is also seen in this example. As teachers, we commonly warn too often, thereby showing the student that we really do not mean what we say. Finally, this case illustrates the value of judicious punishment, whether experienced directly or vicariously, in coping with misbehavior that occurs with a high frequency.

·   ·   ·

Problem: Playground Accidents
Technique: Use of Filmed Models

Mrs. J., a second grade teacher was concerned about the number of playground accidents. Fortunately, most of the accidents were minor in nature, but some could easily have been serious. One of the first things that Mrs. J. did was to present a series of filmstrips and films in which children who played safely had fun and met with no accidents. The filmed models who were careless or intentionally disobeyed rules got hurt or were punished. The teacher also made effective use of her Polaroid camera. Snapshots were made of pupils—particularly the prestigeful ones—who suffered cut lips, or bloody noses, complete with tears and torn clothes, as a result of playground mishaps. Snapshots also were made of well-behaved students enjoying wholesome playground activities. Furthermore, progress charts were instituted with special privileges accorded to the row with the best safety record.

Comment. This case depicts a creative use of filmed models who were rewarded for acceptable behavior and who were punished for unacceptable behavior. The ripple effect seems to be especially great when the injured models are recognized as the students' own classmates.

•   •   •

Problem: Hitting and kicking

Techniques: Social modeling, positive reinforcement, punishment

Jimmy was a kindergartner who kicked and hit when he did not get his own way. The person physically closest to him got it. To change this behavior, the teacher first talked to Jimmy about his behavior, emphasizing how it was not nice to hit someone even though you might be angry with him. She pointed out that she did not hit someone just because she was angry at that person. She just ignored them or told them to leave her alone. Jimmy was specifically instructed to watch how his teacher handled herself when she became mad. He was also seated next to a friend and was encouraged to watch how he handled himself when he became upset.

Cautioned by the school psychologist that social modeling procedures alone might not be effective in inhibiting the aggressive behavior, the teacher decided to combine these with rewards and punishments. Since Jimmy enjoyed painting very much—enough so that he would work on his behavior to keep this privilege—it was used on a contingency basis. The punishment selected consisted of isolating him from other children and from the activities in which he liked to be involved. Through firm and consistent application of these multiple techniques, Jimmy, although still somewhat more emotionally reactive than his classmates, learned to control his behavior and to increase his "frustration tolerance."

Comment. It is often difficult to inhibit behaviors such as aggression which have a strong payoff for the student through modeling alone. Once the child has acquired language, it is possible to rely on verbal modeling cues (telling him what behaviors to copy, for example, the teacher's advice to "ignore them" and "to watch me") as well as overt behavioral ones. Again, live models (his teacher and "buddy") were used. Notice that in this case the teacher directly informed the youngster as to what specific behavior she wanted to change. She did not keep him in the dark as to exactly what constituted objectionable behavior. Rewarding adjacent students is also a useful strategy.

•   •   •

Problem: Enhancing social behavior in preschool isolates

Techniques: Filmed models who were rewarded for approach behaviors

In this study, head teachers in each of nine nursery school classes were asked to select the most withdrawn children in their classes. To qualify for this experiment, the children had to have exhibited extreme withdrawal over a long period of time as judged by their teachers and to have displayed isolate behavior as measured by observations of their behavior. Of the 13 isolates selected, six (four girls and two boys) were assigned to the modeling group, and seven (four girls and three boys) were assigned to the control group. A group of 26 randomly chosen nonisolates were included in the study for the purposes of comparison.

Children in the modeling group were taken to a room where they could watch a "television" program. The child was then left by himself to view a 23-minute sound color film portraying a sequence of 11 scenes in which children interacted in a nursery school setting. In each episode, a child was shown first observing the interaction of others, and then participating in the social activities with rewarding consequences ensuing. The other preschoolers, for instance, offered him play material, talked to him, smiled at him, and generally reacted to his advances toward them in a positive manner. The vigor of the activity and the size of the group were increased gradually. Thus, the initial scenes portrayed very calm activities, for instance, the sharing of a book or toy while just two children were seated at a table. The last scenes, on the other hand, might show as many as six children gleefully heaving play equipment around the room. Because multiple modeling is more efficacious than single modeling, the models varied from scene to scene in terms of sex and age (4 to 7). A narrative sound track, using a "soothing" female voice, was also prepared to accentuate the modeling cues and rewarding consequences associated with the approach or assertive actions of the model.

The control group of isolates viewed a 20-minute film on the acrobatic performances of Marineland dolphins. Observations made immediately following the films indicated that those isolates who had the benefit of symbolic modeling treatment increased their level of social interaction to that of nonisolate nursery school children, whereas control group isolates manifested no changes in their withdrawal behavior. Teacher ratings collected at the end of the school year suggested that only one of the six subjects who had been in the modeling condition was still rated as an isolate in contrast to four of the seven control group subjects (O'Connor, 1969).

Comment. Symbolic modeling coupled with the use of positive reinforcement is a most efficacious means of altering social withdrawal, which reflects both deficits in social skills and the avoidance of feared interpersonal associations. Stated differently, the combination of these two techniques is ideally suited to the transmission of new social skills and to the elimination of social fears. It is easy to envision the eventual use of such films for group use in actual classroom settings. Notice that significant behavioral changes were achieved without developing a therapeutic relationship. This finding would suggest that these materials can be used by teachers as well as by others. School mental health specialists might profitably devote a substantial part of their time and energies to the development of them. Teachers, of course, would also have much to contribute in this regard.

.   .   .

Problem: Shouting in classroom
Techniques: Social modeling, mild reprimand

Many times when primary level students are forced to stay indoors because of inclement weather, they become very high strung. Mrs. C. found that under these circumstances the students would shout and yell at each other during their playtime. In order to restore the noise level to a reasonable point, she would turn off the lights. This meant stop, look, and listen. Then in a soft voice, she would explain that they were interfering with the activities of other classes in the building. Consequently, they would have to settle down somewhat. She found that using a soft voice generally had a calming effect and resulted in the students' using a quiet voice like the teacher. A loud, almost shouting voice, on the other hand, usually caused them to become even noisier.

Comment. This teacher secured student attention—a necessary although not sufficient condition to achieving a modeling effect—by turning off the lights. Her display of calmness and self-restraint served as a cue that inhibited the expression of similar behaviors in the students. Social modeling was not, in this instance, used to teach new behaviors but to serve as a signal for the expression of behaviors that had been previously learned and rewarded. In this case, the teacher used herself as a real life model.

.   .   .

Problem: Development of speech in retarded children
Technique: Modeling and positive reinforcement

The objective of this study was to explore the extent to which the language development of young retarded children could be enhanced through imitation and positive reinforcement. Since linguistic facility is critical to school success, research in this area becomes especially noteworthy. Initially, the children were given a great deal of help to enable them to imitate simple responses (for example, raising the left arm) which were then rewarded with food. Later, more involved actions (for example, moving a hat from the table to the desk) were demonstrated, and successful imitations continued to be rewarded. As the children's imitation became more habitual, several responses were linked together and modeled by the experimenters with positive reinforcement being contingent on the imitation of as many as five separate acts. Up to this point, vocal responses generally had not been imitated when presented alone. However, when vocal responses were introduced at the end of a sequence of motor actions, vocal imitation increased. As vocal imitation rose, the motor actions exhibited by the teacher were shortened trial by trial until eventually only the vocal sounds were presented for imitation. This procedure not only promoted the imitation of vocal responses but established a means through which to teach specific words. Children who had never spoken before—a severe language handicap by any criterion—learned as many as ten functional words after only 20 hours of training (Baer, Peterson, and Sherman, 1967).

Comment. This impressive study exemplifies not only a technique for promoting language development among severely retarded children but provides a potentially useful means for teaching language to young middle class children and to culturally disadvantaged youth. This case also illustrates the value of combining modeling with positive reinforcement to overcome gross deficits in behavior.

SUMMARY

Modeling procedures can provide a shortcut to the learning of new behaviors as well as a means of regulating previously acquired behaviors. As most commonly employed, the teacher serves as a live model allowing his own behavior to set an example of how his students should act. Potent as the teacher is as a model, it is regrettable that an increased use has not been made of influential peer group leaders, especially when attempting to change the behavior of older youth. The use of symbolic models, although largely unexplored by educational personnel, holds considerable promise.

Modeling procedures can have three fundamental effects. They can lead to (1) the establishment of new behaviors, (2) the strengthening or weakening of existent behaviors subjected to punishment, and (3) the facilitating of socially acceptable actions already ingrained in the observer.

Not all individuals are affected in the same way or to the same degree by an exposure to models. Research studies suggest that one's susceptibility to imitative influence varies with (1) the attributes of the model, (2) the attributes of the observer, and (3) the consequences attached to the modeled behavior. Examples of various classroom uses of modeling procedures are given.

REFERENCES

Baer, D.M., Peterson, R.F., and Sherman, J.A. The development of limitation by reinforcing behavioral similarity to a model. *Jr. of Experimental of Behavior*, 1967, **10**, 405–416.

Bandura, A. *Principles of Behavior Modification*. New York: Holt, Rinehart, and Winston, Inc., 1969.

Barnwell, A. and Sechrest, L. Vicarious reinforcement in children at two age levels. *Journal of Educational Psychology*, 1965, **56**, 100–106.

Benton, A. Effects of the timing of negative response consequences on the observational learning of resistance to temptation in children. *Dissertation Abstracts*, 1967, **27**, 2153–2154.

Bronfenbrenner, U. *Two Worlds of Childhood. U.S. and U.S.S.R.* New York: Russell Sage Foundation, 1970.

Chittenden, G. An experimental study in measuring and modifying assertive behavior in young children. *Monographs of the Society for Research in Child Development*, 1942, **7**, 1, No. 31.

Flanders, J. A review of research on imitative behavior. *Psychological Bulletin*, 1968, **69**(5), 316–337.

Gittelman, M. Behavior rehearsal as a technique in child treatment. *Journal of Child Psychology and Psychiatry*, 1965, 251–255.

Gnagey, W. *The Psychology of Discipline in the Classroom*. New York: Macmillan, 1968.

Kounin, J. *Discipline and Group Management in Classrooms*. New York: Holt, Rinehart and Winston, Inc., 1970.

Krumboltz, J., and Thorensen, C. *Behavioral Counseling Cases and Techniques*. New York: Holt, Rinehart and Winston, Inc., 1969.

Loovaas, O., Freitag, L., Nelson, K., and Whelan, C. The establishment of imitation and its use for the development of complex behavior in schizophrenic children. *Behaviour Research and Therapy*, 1967, **5**, 171–181.

Mager, R. *Developing attitude toward learning*. Palo Alto, Calif.: Fearon Publishers, 1968.

O'Connor, R. Modification of social withdrawal through symbolic modeling. *Journal of Applied Behavior Analysis*. 1969, **2**(1), 15–22.

Rosenhan, D., Frederick, F., and Burrowes, A. Preaching and practicing: effects of channel discrepancy on norm internalization. *Child Development*, 1968, 39(1), 291–301.

Walters, R., Parke, R., and Cane, V. Timing of punishment and the observation of consequences to others as determinants of response inhibition. *Journal of Experimental Child Psychology*, 1965, 2, 10–30.

4

Extinction Procedures

Just as a substantial body of research shows that the presentation of rewards can facilitate the acquisition and maintenance of given behaviors, a growing body of literature is demonstrating that extinction—simply removing the reward that usually accompanies the misbehavior—can reduce or eliminate troublesome behaviors. If behavior is learned through the giving of rewards, then it can be unlearned by taking the rewards away. If a given behavior no longer has its intended effect, its frequency tends to diminish.

As Hunter (1967), points out, "We don't keep on doing something that doesn't work." If the troublesome student acts out and nothing happens, he soon gets the message and abandons the particular maladaptive way. In short, simply removing the rewarding consequences of an act constitutes an effective way of weakening it. As we shall learn, this technique has been found effective with a wide variety of behavior.

Despite the simplicity and potency of this principle, teachers often fail to use it to its best advantage. Hopefully, a fuller understanding of the cautions and guidelines regarding the use of this technique will enable teachers to apply it to better advantage.

CAUTIONS AND GUIDELINES

Efficiency and Effectiveness

Although unacceptable behavior can be weakened by the nonrewarded repetition of a response, extinction if used as the sole method is not always the most economical and effective means to produce behavioral change, as we indicate in our discussion below.

Therefore, it is often wise to use extinction in conjunction with other techniques. One especially effective combination involves the simultaneous use of extinction and reward. The teacher might, for instance, ignore the child when he talks out of turn in class but might make a favorable comment about his answers when he speaks out in ways that are consistent with classroom ground rules. For example, "That's a good point, Jim" or "Jim, thank you for waiting your turn," whenever he raises his hand to answer or otherwise waits his turn. If the youngster has not yet learned to raise his hand, the teacher might assist him. For instance, whenever she notices him about to blurt something, she might say in a friendly voice something like, "Jim, did you want to raise your hand to say something?" Or the teacher might say, "Jim, I know you have something you want to say. We'll get to you in just a bit." Then the teacher might call on him in 20 to 30 seconds (gradually this interval could be increased) and say, "Thank you for waiting, Jim. Now, let's hear what you have to say."

A good rule of thumb is to reinforce desirable behaviors, for example, cooperativeness, which are incompatible with and complete with undesirable behaviors, for example, negativistic behavior. A student cannot be both cooperative and negativistic simultaneously. One junior high school teacher after years of yelling, pleading, and belittling, decided to say nothing to the students who forgot to bring the necessary supplies to class (not even a sign of reproach) and to give a daily "A" to book bringers. Within a five-day period, this teacher solved a problem that had annoyed her throughout five years of teaching by positively rewarding a desirable behavior (bringing supplies) which competed with unwanted behavior (forgetting supplies).

The Old Misbehavior Can Return

We should point out that the term extinction is probably a misnomer, since extinguished behavior is displaced rather than permanently lost. Moreover, if the original undesirable misbehavior is again reinforced, it is often easily reinstated. This difficulty can be overcome through the use of additional extinction trials, however. For example, one teacher had, for all practical purposes, eliminated tantrum behavior in Jane, a third grade student, by ignoring her temper outbursts. The teacher was ill for a week. On her return she found that Jane was up to her old tricks again. The teacher later confirmed her suspicions, namely, that the substitute teacher had inadvertently strengthened tantrum behavior by attending to it. Nevertheless, the regular teacher again was able to reduce these episodes to a minimal frequency through the reinstatement of her ignoring policy.

What should the teacher do when old habits reoccur after they have been supposedly eliminated? Although you may be inclined to blow your top and thereby to reinforce the misbehavior, you should simply lay the unwanted behavior to rest once again by withholding reinforcement, that is, you should undertake another series of extinction trials. Fortunately, the unwanted behavior can usually be more readily extinguished on the second series of extinction trials.

Occasional Reward

One of the primary factors in the reappearance of undesirable behavior is occasional or intermittent reward. As noted earlier in our discussion of intermittent reinforcement behaviors, troublesome or otherwise, once these behaviors have been established, they can be maintained or even strengthened even though they are only occasionally reinforced. What sometimes happens is that many deviant behaviors, for example, talking out loud in class, are occasionally reinforced either directly or vicariously and are thereby set up on an intermittent reinforcement schedule. Thus, instead of abolishing the behavior via extinction as intended, there is a rise in the frequency and intensity of deviant responses via intermittent reinforcement. On some occasions, a given teacher may be inconsistent in his ignoring of a certain behavior. For instance, he may become angry when the disorderly student talks out loud in class and, consequently, may pay attention to the behavior by scolding. On other occasions, there may be inconsistency between teachers. This type of inconsistency is most likely to occur in elementary schools in conjunction with team-taught courses and in junior and senior high school where students typically have several teachers. Remember that any rewards given during the extinction process will reinstate the misbehavior and, frequently, at a higher level than if extinction had not been attempted (Bandura, 1969).

Inability to Ignore Misbehavior

This brings us to a related point, namely, that it is especially difficult for teachers to ignore behavior deviations. We are good detectives and we quickly spot (and attend to) rule violations. It is as though we are compelled to respond to misbehavior. "George, get back to your seat." "Mary, you've been at the pencil sharpener long enough." "Bob, stop pestering your neighbors and get back to work." "Tom, do you always have to be moving around in your desk?" "Barry, how long are you going to keep tapping that pencil?" "Carol, sit up straight." "Bill, watch your feet." "Steve, scoot your chair over." As you know now, teacher attention can often strengthen the undesirable behavior. Although teachers have little difficulty in grasping the value of ignoring (and thereby of removing the reward for the deviant behavior), they have considerable difficulty in implementing this idea. As one teacher related, "As a practice teacher, I vowed that I would not hen like my supervising teaching but found myself doing it too once I got on the job." Being aware of the value of ignoring is one matter, and practicing to ignore is quite another. Ignoring requires rigorous self-control.

If teachers are to derive the maximum benefit from extinction procedures, they must learn not to respond to all undesirable behavior.[1] In all likelihood, many classroom transgressions could be safely ignored. Motor behaviors such as getting out of the seat, standing up, wandering around the room, and moving chairs could probably be ignored. Irrelevant verbalizations or noises such as conversations with others, answering without raising one's hand, crying, whistling, and coughing also can fall into the category of behaviors to which the teacher should not respond. Oppositional tactics, for example, negativism, represent another major class of behaviors to which no heed should be paid (Madsen et. al., 1968). The teacher, even though he might initially feel uncomfortable, will do a more adequate job of managing classroom behavior if he can learn to avoid responding to certain misbehaviors. Remember that teacher disapproval can strengthen deviant behavior, whereas ignoring it can weaken such behavior by removing the pay off. The student has to learn that unacceptable behavior is worth nothing.

Should a teacher ignore all undesirable behavior? If not, how will he know what behaviors to ignore? The general guidelines that follow should prove of value in helping teachers answer these questions. There are certain types of behavior that the teacher cannot ignore. Included among them are behaviors that are injurious to self or others and inappropriate behaviors for which the teacher cannot for various reasons remove the reward, that is, self-rewarding behaviors and behaviors rewarded by the peer group. Hunter (1967) suggests that if a given misbehavior is relatively new, one can probably ignore it. On the other hand, if the misbehavior occurs with a high degree of consistency and is of long standing,

---

[1] Because it is unlikely that a teacher will ignore all instances of a given misbehavior, extinction procedures should be combined with the positive reinforcement of acceptable behaviors.

extinction procedures may prove inadequate. If the misbehavior happens frequently and is of long standing, one can be reasonably sure that it is being reinforced. Either other social agents such as the peer group are making these deviances worth the student's while or his behavior is rewarding in and of itself, for example, sleeping in class, laughing, and hitting. As we indicate later, it might well be necessary to use some form of punishment to deal effectively with behavior that is intense and/or frequent. For now, remember that ignoring works only when the reward is attention. When systematic teacher ignoring fails, it is likely that the misbehavior is being maintained by something other than teacher attention, and that some other change in the classroom environment will be needed to discourage the behavior.

Peer Rewarded Behavior

Some comments relative to peer group extinction deserve mention at this point. Conversations with and observations of teachers indicate that they frequently do not come to grips with the problem of the peer group. More often than not, teachers allow the peer group to reinforce undesirable behavior. For instance, if a boy clowns in class and three to four other students generally respond with laughter, teachers rarely enlist the assistance of these students in extinguishing the undesired behavior. Just as peer group rewards can serve as powerful strengtheners of behavior, group extinction procedures also can serve as powerful weakeners of behavior, as is illustrated in the case of George, a first grader who was described as immature, disruptive, and poorly motivated by his teacher. The following announcement was made to George's class.

> George does not learn as much as he can because he has really not learned how to sit still and work. This is a "how-to-work-box" that will help him to practice working. When he sits still and works, the light flashes up here like this (demonstrates) and the counter clicks. When that happens it means that George has earned one M&M candy. When he is all done working today, we will take all of the candy he earns and divide it up among all of you. If you want George to earn a lot of candy, then don't pay any attention to him if he acts silly, talks to you, or gets up out of his seat. O.K.? Now, lets see how much candy George can earn. (Patterson, 1969).

Although every teacher might not have a "how to work box" nor wish to pass out M&M candy, he could still make use of group extinction procedures by finding incentives more natural to the classroom setting which could be used for the peer group's ignoring of inappropriate behavior. Again, notice the simultaneous use of positive reinforcement and extinction procedures.

Self-reinforcing Behavior

Occasionally the reward for misbehavior comes from the act itself. Consequently, it is sometimes extremely difficult to keep maladaptive behaviors from being reinforced. For instance, the aggressive pupil who kicks the teacher or a classmate cannot help but be reinforced by the look of pain on the victim's face. Furthermore, even if the victim somehow manages to keep a straight face, the kicker knows that he has inflicted pain, and this knowledge in itself can be reinforcing. Looking out the window, having a good belly laugh, or having a conquering hero daydream are all intrinsically rewarding. When dealing with behavior that contains its own satisfactions, it is necessary to punish the undesirable behavior to suppress it temporarily and to reward incompatible positive behaviors. For example, the aggressive student may have to relinquish certain classroom privileges, such as playing with his peers, when he acts out. Yet, every effort should be made to reward his cooperative or friendly interactions.

Intense Misbehavior

There are also situations in which we cannot wait for a behavior to fizzle out through repeated nonreward. This limitation is particularly characteristic of situations wherein the dangers of emotional contagion and severe injury to self or others are distinct possibilities. In these cases, immediate action is called for, and some form of punishment (for example, isolation or physical restraint) is probably the method of choice.

Original Misbehavior Increases

The teacher should fully expect that misbehavior, if it does not increase in frequency or in intensity, will remain at a high level during the initial stages of the extinction process. The old adage that things will get worse before they get better certainly pertains here. Temper tantrums may well soar to frightening intensities, initially mild dependency demands may culminate in a sharp kick in the shins, and negative attention-getting behavior may assume increasingly ludicrous forms (Bandura, 1969). This state of affairs should not discourage the teacher, since the initial rise in undesired behavior is a sign that the extinction process is working. As the vigorous misbehavior proves unsuccessful, it will gradually taper off and alternative ways of behavior will emerge.

The systematic application of extinction procedures is essential. The teacher must be consistent and must stick to his guns, since the troublesome child believes on the basis of his past experience that he will get his way if he persists. He has hope of attaining the customary reward for his misbehavior. Eventually, he figures, the teacher will give in, accidently or intentionally. Since the student has had luck with his tactics before, he is going to try them again and again. The message to teachers is clear —stick to your guns.

New Misbehaviors Sometimes Emerge

The extinction of a given maladaptive behavior constitutes no guarantee in and of itself that desirable behavior will automatically appear. As dominant modes of behavior are extinguished, the student will use alternative courses of action that have proved successful on previous occasions in similar circumstances. The use of extinction alone poses no special problems provided that the alternative responses in the student's repertoire are acceptable to the teacher. A problem does arise, however, when the new responses are also maladaptive. If this situation arises, the teacher may be faced with the laborious task of extinguishing a long succession of unacceptable behavior patterns. For example, one student turned to verbal impersonations of the teacher after his pantomiming had gone unrewarded. It was necessary, therefore, for the teacher to extinguish the verbal impersonations too. The teacher can avoid the problems associated with extinguishing a long succession of inappropriate behaviors by combining extinction procedures with other methods that foster more effective modes of adjustment (Bandura, 1969).

Because teachers have not always taken into account the above-mentioned cautions and guidelines, they have sometimes become discouraged in their use of this technique. We have seen many teachers become disheartened in trying to implement the school counselor's advice not to reward maladaptive behaviors. What usually happens, unless the above precautions are taken, is that the teachers' efforts to extinguish unacceptable student behaviors themselves undergo extinction. A summary of cautions and guidelines is presented in Table 4.1

In conclusion, the rate and effectiveness of extinction as an intervention technique are dictated by several factors. Among them are (1) the irregularity with which the maladaptive behavior has been rewarded in the past (recall that the occasional reward of an established behavior

TABLE 4.1

A Summary of Cautions and Guidelines Regarding

Extinction Procedures

Caution	Guideline
Not always economical or effective if used alone	Combine extinction with other methods, especially the rewarding of incompatible behaviors.
Old habits can reoccur	Lay problem to rest again through an additional extinction series.
Occasional reward	Be consistent. Make sure you are not the reinforcing agent.
Inability to ignore unwanted behavior	Practice not responding to all misbehavior.
Peer rewarded behavior	Enlist support of peer group.
Self-reinforcing behavior	Combine extinction with other methods such as reward of competing responses and punishment.
Intense misbehavior	Some form of punishment may be the method of choice.
Original misbehavior increases	Expect this initial rise. Continue to apply extinction procedures systematically.
New misbehaviors sometimes emerge	Combine extinction procedures with other methods that foster desired behavior (social modeling, reward).

makes extinction a more arduous process); (2) the ease with which the teacher can identify and remove the rewards that are maintaining the maladaptive behavior; (3) the availability of alternative modes of behaving in the student's repertoire or in those opened up to him by the teacher; (4) the amount of effort needed to misbehave (theoretically, one might expect violent, extended tantrum behavior to extinguish more readily than whining behavior, since the former requires more energy and effort on the student's part); (5) the student's level of deprivation during the extinction process (the class clown, for example, after a short illness that kept him out of school might well relinquish his need for peer approval—social deprivation level—is higher now that he missed his buddies); (6) the extent to which extinction procedures are combined with other behavior modification methods such as positive reinforcement, social modeling, punishment, and desensitization; (7) the teacher's ability to ignore certain kinds of misbehavior, and (8) the teacher's ability to apply extinction techniques in a consistent and systematic way.

EXAMPLES OF EXTINCTION

Problem: Constant blurting out behavior

Agent: Teacher

Methods Used: Extinction, Social Modeling and Reward

A second grade teacher was concerned because she had a class of 25 overeager children who consistently blurted and yelled out their answers instead of waiting and raising their hands. In talking with the counselor about the problem, the teacher was encouraged to ignore all calling out of answers and to refrain from giving any facial or verbal recognition to the child who called an answer out. The children who raised their hands were called on and acknowledged with "Billy has his hand up and is waiting to answer the question," or "Sally has her hand up and is being considerate to the class." To encourage hand-raising behavior, the teacher reinforced the behavior every time it occurred with some comment as to how patient or considerate the student was to the class. As hand raising increased, the number of reinforcements needed decreased. If the student did not know the answers, he was given prompts so as to increase the likelihood that he would be rewarded for having raised his hand. If it was not possible to elicit the answer even with prompts, the teacher praised the student for making a good try. The teacher found that many members of the class who never answered before were now raising their hands and were thereby given more opportunities to respond correctly and to contribute to class discussions. The teacher could now spend a greater amount of time listening to the comments of her youngsters instead of always reminding them to raise their hands. The class was quieter, yet the quality and quantity of class participation had improved.

Comment. (1) Note that the teacher did not reinforce blurting out behavior with either nonverbal recognition, for example, facial expressions, or verbal recognition. Although many teachers realize in retrospect that they have inadvertently rewarded undesirable behavior through verbal attention, they often overlook the reinforcement value of nonverbal forms of attention (staring, frowning, pointing one's finger, sighing, shaking one's head "no"). (2) The case also illustrates the shift from regular to irregular reinforcement. When the students were learning to raise their hands, they were rewarded as often as possible for doing so. Once hand-raising behavior was learned, the teacher gave rewards on an irregular or occasional basis. (3) Again we see the use made of the incompatible response strategy—when one raises his hand, he usually does not blurt out. (4) This case offers another example of how behavior modfication can be used with groups as well as with individuals.

• • •

Problem: Aggressiveness and hyperactivity

Techniques: Extinction by teacher and peers, use of rewarded models

Danny was a five-year-old enrolled in a Head Start class. After remaining on the fringes of the group for a week, he became more aggressive and hyperactive. He would spill another child's orange juice, knock over another's tower made of blocks, throw the ball over the playground fence, threw away clean napkins to be used for snacks, and engage in a variety of other impulsive and destructive behaviors. He was always promptly scolded for his misbehavior.

A case conference was held and the teachers, although reluctant, agreed to ignore his inappropriate behaviors. In keeping with this strategy, the teachers ignored Danny when he would run in the opposite direction instead of coming indoors. As one might suspect, the teachers wondered whether he would come back. At first, he would run outside the fence, laughing and yelling in an effort to attract attention. Initially, some children would try to call the teacher's attention to Danny's tactics. On these occasions, the teacher would simply change the topic of conversation. She would, for example, express curiosity about what their snack for that day was to be and would continue on into the classroom. After a few seconds, Danny would appear at the door and shout, "Teacher, look at me!" Some of the students turned to look at him, but the teacher continued talking about the subject at hand as they munched their snacks. The teacher, for purposes of imitation, provided the students with a model who does not pay attention to inappropriate behavior. A combination of both teacher and peer extinction procedures was now underway. The next day, Danny came indoors with the other youngsters even though he was the last one in. He did not wash his hands or eat his snack but, instead, went to the back of the room to build high towers of blocks only to send them tumbling to the floor. He would look at the teacher each time he smashed a tower. Both the teacher and the other children ignored him.

On the third day, Danny was again the last one to come in, but this time he managed to arrive at the table just before the end of snack time. The cookies had been eaten, but the teacher offered him some juice which he drank. He forgot to put his napkin in the basket but this "oversight" was ignored.

On the fourth day, Danny came indoors, washed his hands, and went to the snack table. The head teacher seated him and included him in the conversation but did not make a big affair of his joining the others for a snack for fear that any form of conspicuous reinforcement might call more attention to his usual misbehavior than to his accepted behavior. Danny's behavior became more constructive, and the teacher rewarded his efforts by paying attention to him. She encouraged him, for example, by statements such as "I like the colors you are using" or "Your picture is interesting, Danny. Tell me about it." Within two weeks, Danny's behavior changed from disruptive to cooperative and from destructive to constructive (Vance, 1969).

Comment. This case study, in addition to illustrating the effectiveness of extinction procedures also highlights the benefits that can accrue from a combination of techniques—in this case, extinction, positive reward, and punishment (missing the snack) and the provision of appropriate models.

●   ●   ●

Problem: Irresponsible, immature behavior

Technique: Combination of reward and extinction

Extinction procedures also have been used effectively with older students as is shown in the case of Jerry, a junior high school student who was continually tardy to classes, forgot class materials, engaged in baby talk, wore unusual hats, emitted noises resembling various machines, and blamed others for his difficulties. At the counselor's suggestion, Jerry's teachers and mother ignored his baby talk, his strange noises, and unique attire. Under the regimen, Jerry showed slow but steady improvement, and by the end of the year, he no longer wore bizarre clothes or made strange noises. His baby talk and projection of blame onto others were still evident but they seemed less frequent. His grades improved, he was rarely tardy for class, and he remembered his class materials. His teachers generally were satisfied with his progress. Thus, through the use of extinction and positive reinforcement procedures, Jerry came to assume responsibility for his classroom behavior (Castle, 1969).

Comment. This study illustrates how the manipulation of the student's environment can promote greater self-direction. It also depicts the value of a close relationship between parents and school authorities. Again, we see the counselor serving in a consultative capacity to the teacher.

• • •

Problem: Control of masturbatory play and constant finger contact with the other youngsters

Agent: Teacher

Methods used: Extinction and positive rewards

Mary is a six-year-old mongoloid child in a special education program. The teacher was concerned about the frequency of her masturbatory play and constant finger contact with other youngsters. These behaviors were most frequent during unstructured activities such as snack time or play period. During snack time one hand would be under the table or poking another child.

In a conference with the school psychologist it was decided that:

1. Mary and the other children would not be able to have their snack until both hands were on the table and they were quiet.
2. Mary's physical contact with the children would be ignored as much as possible.
3. Mary would be attended to when she was not engaging in either masturbatory or physical contact behavior.

After a week on this program, it was noticed that during snack time the children were placing both hands on the table and, consequently, Mary was not engaged in masturbatory play. Physical contacts decreased because they were being ignored by the teacher and did not disrupt the activities of the class as it had previously. Behaviors, for example, playing with another child or working on completing a puzzle or assignment, that were without physical contact, increased in frequency as they were periodically reinforced by favorable comments from the teacher.

Comment. Again, we observe the effective use made of the incompatible response strategy. Mary could not masturbate at snack time because both hands had to be on the table in order to receive and to keep the snack. Desirable behaviors (keeping hands off of others, and keeping hands on the table during snack time) were strengthened and unacceptable behaviors (masturbatory play and finger contact with others) were weakened primarily through ignoring. The sensitive reader probably also detected the use of peers as rewarded models for Mary to imitate, that is, having other students keep both hands on the table and rewarding them for this behavior. The importance of identifying situations or conditions leading up to the misbehavior is also highlighted in this study. Because the teacher noticed that masturbatory play was most common during unstructured activities, she was in a much better position to plan ways to cope with this kind of deviant behavior.

.   .   .

Problem: Mimicking idiosyncrasies of the teacher
Method: Removing teacher and peer attention

Polly was very adept at mimicking her teacher's idiosyncrasies, for example, hand gestures and facial expressions, and this behavior was reinforced by the teacher's tirades and the applause reaction of classmates. The more the teacher tried to "lecture" Polly about her behavior, the greater the frequency and exaggeration of the mimicking behavior. Another teacher on overhearing the comments of the students about the show being put on by Polly, tactfully talked to the teacher and was able to convince her that her vehement lectures were actually strengthening Polly's undesirable behavior. Polly's teacher was advised to withdraw the reinforcement for this type of misbehavior by ignoring the imitations. Along with this neutral response, Polly was moved from the front of the room (away from the center stage) to the back of the room. Thus she was deprived of an audience.

At first, Polly's performances increased and changed from pantomiming to verbal impersonations, but without the subsequent reinforcement of an angry teacher and peer group approval the imitations quickly vanished.

Comment. The following points are noteworthy: (1) It is imperative in cases like this that the teacher remove the reward coming from the peer group. If peer group rewards could not have been removed and Polly's objectionable behavior had continued, the inclusion of punishment procedures, for example, time-out periods, might well have been incorporated into the plans for altering Polly's behavior. (2) Extinction procedures call for the utmost consistency on the part of the teacher, since occasional reward serves to maintain habitual behaviors. (3) Notice that Polly's misbehavior actually rose and changed from pantomiming to verbal impersonation before succumbing to extinction procedures.

.   .   .

Problem: Gaining attention through passive-aggressive behavior toward the teacher
Extinction: Withdrawing teacher attention

Toni was able to fluster and to irritate her teacher by playing the role of "the dumb, slow student." Toni would constantly ask questions the answers to which were evident. For example, after the teacher had given the pages of the assignment out loud and had written them on the board, Toni would ask what pages the assignment was on? When the teacher curtly asked her to repeat the assignment pages, Toni was able to answer her own question.

She also manipulated her teacher to give her a negative, flustered response by pretending not to be able to do an assignment in which she had been previously successful. This behavior was exemplified by her reading assignment. Toni was called on to read some words, she read them very well, and the teacher praised her reading. The other students did not do nearly as well as Toni, so for the next day's assignment, the class was to study the words and to be able to read them correctly. The next day, when Toni was called to read the same words, she faltered and pretended that she could not read the words. The teacher knowing that she knew the words, became irritated with her and reassigned them as homework. Toni seemed to thrive on the teacher's inability to handle the situation.

The teacher, realizing that her irritation and curt comments were precisely what Toni wanted, decided that she would simply call on another student when Toni pretended that she did not know the answer. When Toni blurted out one of her "questions," the teacher would continue her explanation, repeating the directions and giving no direct attention to Toni. Under this program, the teacher noticed that the attention-getting behaviors were slowly being extinguished because they no longer "paid-off" by the teacher's flustered appearance. Toni was better able to start and to complete assignments now without her previous pretense and questioning actions.

Comment. This is a good example of how teacher attention can sometimes strengthen the very behavior we want to eliminate. The reader can probably imagine how difficult it was for Toni's teacher to ignore such taunting behavior. Learning not to respond requires considerable restraint and practice.

*   *   *

Problem: Chronic fighting with other boys on the playground
Agent: Child himself
Method: Extinction combined with reinforcement of a competing response

Jimmy was referred to the school social worker for being a chronic fighter on the playground. He was 10 years and seven months old and was in the sixth grade. Jimmy's fighting was so habitual that he was suspended from school on four occasions during a five-month period (in order to be suspended, a student had to receive five misconduct slips for fighting in one week). Every misconduct slip that Jimmy received was for fighting on the playground. Because the fights were always provoked by the other boys calling him names, the teacher felt that if Jimmy could ignore these remarks, the name-calling would decrease and his fighting would be curtailed.

It was decided that Jimmy himself should be the agent who would be actively involved in extinguishing the name-calling behavior. Instead of reacting with anger, Jimmy was instead told to ignore the taunts, to act as if he had never heard them. Jimmy had already been told that the other boys would probably not call him names if he would not pay attention to them, but he was still unable to control his temper. It was decided that he could not adhere to the extinction procedure unless he were to make an active response that was incompatible with his usual response (fighting) to name-calling. Accordingly, he was asked to write the name-caller's name on a sheet of paper which he carried in his pocket. This procedure was to serve as an incompatible response to fighting and to give him a record of who was doing the most name calling.

Data collected for eight consecutive weeks after the initiation of extinction procedures showed that Jimmy's fighting behavior had completely disappeared. The name-calling responses dropped gradually, and within two weeks they had been completely extinguished (Goens, 1969).

Comment. The question arises as to why Jimmy was able to ignore name-calling at this time when he had been unable to do so in the past. Two possible explanations were advanced: (1) he was now required to perform a response that competed with fighting. One cannot fight and write at the same time. (2) This time he was told that name-calling would not disappear immediately, but that it would die out gradually if he continued to ignore it consistently.

•   •   •

Problem: Tattling

Extinction: The use of ignoring and rewarding by school authorities

School personnel found that tattling was becoming very common among children in the primary grades. Students seemed to delight in telling about others' affairs. They would tattle to the teacher, the building secretary, the custodian, the principal, and the teacher's aid. "Jack pushed Mary." "Tom and Chuck are throwing snowballs." "Sam took the forbidden route to the lunchroom." "A bunch of guys are playing ball where they're not supposed to be." "Peter made a mess in the bathroom." School authorities would sometimes take action against the student who was tattled on but, generally, they sent the tattler back to his room or desk and told him not to tattle anymore. School personnel found that by listening to the tales and by occasionally acting in accordance with the stories, the tattling behavior was increasing and becoming uncontrollable.

To limit the number of incidents reported, the teachers first informed their classes that they would watch the room and that they would not act on any incident that they had not personally observed. They then ignored all the tales that were reported to them and rewarded the students when they were able to resolve their own interpersonal difficulties. When students approached them to tattle, they would say nothing to the child either acting as if the tattler were not there or else turn their back to him (listening is reinforcing). Teachers did not tell the tattlers to mind their own business or to go back to their seats. The tattlers soon got the message. The teachers found that the tattling behavior was reduced, that the children were more able to play cooperatively with each other, and that they settled their own differences instead of running immediately to the teacher.

Comment. The combination of reward and extinction is depicted in this case study. The basic strategy was to weaken inappropriate behavior (tattling) and to strengthen desirable behavior (getting along with others and handling one's own disputes). Again we witness the use of incompatible responses, that is, one does not tattletale when he resolves his own conflict with his buddies. Finally, the case illustrates that various school personnel can quickly learn and effectively apply extinction techniques.

* * *

Problem: Academic errors

Method: Removal of teacher attention

Extinction procedures have also been used to modify unacceptable academic behavior. For example, one child when asked to spell a word that he had previously studied, would make faces, mumble, and pause momentarily. The teacher would respond by spending considerable time in assisting the boy to sound out the word until it was spelled correctly. Despite the teacher's individual attention, the boy's spelling failed to improve. In retrospect, it was suspected that teacher attention served to maintain his spelling errors. To correct this situation, the teacher ignored his misspellings but paid attention to his correct spellings. Every time the boy misspelled a word, he would look at the teacher. The teacher would not respond, however. After exposure to this technique, the number of incorrect words decreased as did the amount of time needed to write them correctly. When ten words were spelled correctly, the boy received an "A" as well as social attention from the teacher. Within a month, misspellings were virtually nonexistent and he continued to make academic progress (Zimmerman and Zimmerman, 1962).

Comment. It is interesting to observe that academic errors, much like undesirable social behaviors, can be maintained through teacher attention and can be extinguished by the removal of this attention.

• • •

Problem: Eliminating troublesome transition periods
Method: Ignoring and punishment
   One fifth grade teacher frequently found herself fighting with her class to get them ready for events such as recess, gym, lunch, and dismissal time. Although she threatened, yelled, and assisted them by getting things put away, helping them line up, and the like, their behavior failed to improve. In thinking this situation through, she realized that she was actually strengthening their misbehavior with her attention. Hence, she decided on a new strategy—to ignore them, even if it took all the patience she had. The next day, she simply told them once to put their things away and get lined up to go outside. As expected, the usual talking and procrastination occurred. The teacher said nothing. Instead, she busied herself at the desk doing some paperwork that she had to finish. That first day, it took five minutes before they were ready to go out. The students started disciplining one another. "Hush up, so we can get going." The next day, it took them about three minutes. Within a week, the teacher had succeeded in eliminating these troublesome transition periods from her day. Moreover, she taught her students to become more self-reliant.

Comment. This case exemplifies the combined use of extinction and punishment (taking away part of their recess, gym period, and the like).

• • •

Problem: Oppositional behavior
Method: Ignoring, positive reward and social modeling
   Argumentive Al always had negative comments to make, for example, "Oh, that won't work." He delighted in antagonizing the teacher by dis-

rupting class discussions. Rather than being trapped into these attention-getting maneuvers, the teacher intentionally ignored Al when he made negative comments or simply took the thunder out of his oppositional remarks by saying, "Oh, Al, you want to argue about everything." She would then quickly shift her attention and would listen attentively to those students who offered positive and supportive ideas.

Comment. This teacher used a combination of ignoring, positive reward (listening to acceptable comments), and social modeling (I do not pay attention to troublemakers, but I do reward those who have constructive ideas).

• • •

Problem: Frequent trips to the teacher's desk
Method: Extinction plus positive reward of a competing response

Jane, a second grader, would average ten to twelve trips daily to the teacher's desk. One common excuse for coming to the desk was to ask permission to sharpen her pencil. The teacher played into Jane's hand by talking with her whenever she came up to the desk. Finally, she was advised by the school psychologist to ignore Jane completely *every* time she came up. There was to be no conversation whatsoever at the teacher's desk, not even eye contact. Jane was to get attention, however, when she did remain in her seat. Within a month, the frequency of Jane's attention-getting behavior had diminished to the point that it no longer posed a problem for the teacher.

Comment. In keeping with the practice of systematic ignoring, the teacher should attempt to ignore all students who come to her desk in order to avoid providing students like Jane with a vicarious sense of reward. Since total ignoring of any given misbehavior is often impossible, it is essential that the teacher reward desirable behaviors that compete with the unwanted behavior.

SUMMARY

Extinction is a behavior modification technique designed to weaken undesirable behavior simply by discontinuing the rewarding consequences. To facilitate the modification of deviant behaviors, it is best to combine extinction procedures with other techniques such as positive reinforcement, social modeling, and at times punishment. The combination of extinction and positive reward is not only effective but it reduces the unpleasant emotional side effects associated with not being rewarded.

Remember that the course of extinction for deeply entrenched behaviors is apt to be more difficult after intermittent reinforcement. Because of the unpleasant nature of much deviant behavior, it is extremely difficult for the teacher not to attend to (and thereby reinforce) it. The teacher, to be most effective, must practice ignoring certain behaviors, since ignoring them helps a child to forget behaviors. Obviously, all behaviors cannot be extinguished by this procedure. For example, the weakening of self-rewarding behaviors like aggression warrants the use of other techniques as well. Teachers also must be prepared to enforce consequences (pleasant and/or unpleasant) when certain members of the peer group reward disruptive behavior in a given student.

Inconsistency means that unacceptable modes of behavior will provide occasional rewards and, consequently, will strengthen misbehavior. Systematic application of extinction procedures is imperative. Do not be disheartened when misbehavior intensifies following the initiation of extinction procedures. The student simply wants to prove to himself and to others that his misbehavior will pay off if he is persistent enough. If you are consistent, his misbehavior will gradually diminish and other behaviors will replace them. Properly used, extinction strategies can promote the student's personal and academic adjustment as well as make your day more enjoyable.

REFERENCES

Bandura, A. Principles of Behavior Modification. New York: Holt, Rinehart and Winston, Inc., 1969.

Castle, W. Assuming responsibility for appropriate classroom behavior in J. Krumboltz and C. Thoresen (eds.), Behavioral Counseling. New York: Holt, Rinehart and Winston, Inc., 1969, pp. 33–36.

Goens, B. The effects of teaching a physically aggressive child operant techniques. School Applications of Learning Theory, 1969, 1, 17–21.

Hunter, M. Reinforcement. El Segundo, California: TIP Publications, 1967.

Madsen, C., Becker, W., and Thomas, D. Rules, praise and ignoring: elements of elementary classroom control, Journal of Applied Behavioral Analysis, 1968, 1, 139–150.

Patterson, G. Teaching parents to be behavior modifiers in the classroom in J. Krumboltz and C. Thoresen (eds.), Behavioral Counseling. New York: Holt, Rinehart and Winston, Inc., 1969, pp. 155–161.

Vance, B. Modifying hyperactive and aggressive behavior in J. Krumboltz and C. Thoresen (eds.), Behavioral Counseling. New York: Holt, Rinehart and Winston, Inc., 1969, pp. 30–33.

Zimmerman, E., and Zimmerman, J. The alteration of behavior in a special classroom situation. Journal of Experimental Analysis of Behavior, 1962, 5, 59–60.

5

Punishment: A New Look

CAUTIONS AND GUIDELINES

Punishment has been widely used by parents and teachers in their attempts to modify misbehavior when it is frequent and/or intense. However, the use of negative consequences to change behavior generally has been disavowed on the grounds that its use produces a variety of undesirable side effects. Traditionally, certain specific objections have been raised against the use of punishment, or aversive control, as it is frequently called, as a behavior modification technique, and the cautions and limitations that we shall presently discuss suggest that if punishment is to be used as a means of changing behavior, its use should be judiciously applied. As Bandura (1969) notes, "Because of the varied and complex effects of punishment, aversive control, particularly when socially mediated, must be employed with care and skill in programs of behavioral change."

Despite the limitations associated with this technique, many psychologists now contend that certain negative sanctions, if properly applied, can assist in eliminating detrimental patterns of adjustment. As we shall see shortly, the undesirable by-products are not necessarily inherent in punishment but stem from the faulty fashion in which it is applied. Indeed, considerable human behavior is changed and maintained by natural aversive consequences without any ill effects. To avoid painful consequences, we put on warm clothes to protect against the cold, we walk along the side of the road, we run from falling objects, and so forth. We engage in a great deal of behavior simply to avoid pain, and our personalities do not become warped as a result. Few would criticize the use

99

of punishment in teaching young children to stay out of busy streets, to keep their hands off of hot stoves, or to refrain from inserting metal objects in electric wall sockets (Bandura, 1969).

The use of punishment as an intervention technique is most likely necessary in that it is impossible to guide children effectively through the use of only positive reinforcement and extinction. Ausubel (1961), among others, rejects the idea that only "positive" forms of discipline are beneficial. He points out that a child does not come to regard rudeness as an undesirable form of behavior simply by reinforcing respect for others. As Ausubel (1961) asserts, "it is impossible for children to learn what is *not* approved and tolerated simply by generalizing in reverse from the approval they receive for the behavior that is acceptable."

SOME LIMITATIONS AND SOLUTIONS

In this section, we examine some of the drawbacks associated with the use of punishment as a means of promoting desirable changes in student behavior. Attention will also be directed to the overcoming of these problems. Let us at this point consider five of the most common criticisms and see how we might avoid the pitfalls that stem from this technique.

Transitory Effects

Laboratory studies that have been conducted on animals suggested that punishment does not eliminate the maladaptive response. Instead, it merely slowed down the rate at which the troublesome behaviors were emitted. How many times have you scolded a student, kept him in from recess, retained him after school, put him out in the hall, threatened to lower his grade, or sent him to the principal's office only to find that he engages in the very same misbehavior after a short while? Discouraging, isn't it?

How can the teacher who uses punishment achieve more lasting results? One strategy that is designed to promote a durable elimination involves the combined use of punishment and reward. Various research studies indicate that this combination is much more effective and efficient than the use of punishment alone. Punishment reminds the student what not to do. The reward of appropriate alternative behaviors tells the student what he should do. If a student pushes another to get his way and the teacher scolds, the child knows that he should not shove. But he still does not know appropriate ways to get what he wants. Together, these two techniques become an effective duo. The basic rationale is to hold undesirable behaviors in abeyance so that we can establish more acceptable behaviors through positive reward and/or modeling. That is, we suppress the undesirable behaviors through punishment until some desirable behavior has a chance of becoming strong enough to replace the unacceptable responses. Once the newly acquired acceptable behavior becomes firmly entrenched, the teacher might well be able to remove the punishment. How is this possible? Because the new behavior is always or frequently rewarded, whereas the old misbehavior is relinquished in that it no longer pays off for the student. For example, cooperative and sharing behavior, which is now strongly reinforced by the teacher and class, produces attention and acceptance, whereas antisocial behavior and selfishness results in the student being sent into isolation. Hunter's (1967) analogy is germane:

> With a child who is having problems, it is as if you had a strong runner (undesirable behavior) and a weak runner (desirable behavior) racing for a prize. The strong runner is used to winning so you hold him back (punishment) and let the weak runner win the race and get the prize (positive reinforcement). You keep on doing this until the weak runner has had so much practice his legs are getting very strong and he enjoys running for the prize. When you think he has practiced enough that he can beat the strong runner, you let go of the formerly strong runner you have been holding back (remove punishment) so they can both race. As the previously weak runner (desirable behavior) keeps on winning (positive reinforcement), the formerly strong runner (undesirable behavior) gives up (is extinguished) because he never wins anything (no reinforcement). He won't give up as long as he is held back but if he keeps on losing (no reinforcement), he will.

Let us consider the case of a whining student. Because whining is a deeply ingrained characteristic in this girl and occurs so frequently, it may well prove necessary to use punishment to suppress this behavior. "Mary, if you whine, you will have to leave the game" might be a consistently enforced sanction whenever whining behavior crops up. As soon as Mary displays the desired behavior, namely, being a good sport who does not whine when things do not go her way, the teacher should immediately reinforce her: "That's a girl, Mary. You're being such a good sport about things that you can go first this time." Once "being a good sport" behavior becomes rather common for Mary, we might try removing the negative sanction (leaving the game) applied to whining. If the whining behavior occurs then, we could simply extinguish it by allowing it to come out unreinforced while we continue to reward "good sportsmanship" behaviors. We would simply ignore her when she whined and praise her for her courteous interpersonal relations and graceful acceptance of consequences associated with difficult situations (Hunter, 1967).

One form of punishment that combines punishment and reward and thereby offers the student a sense of direction is restitution, a technique long used by teachers. A certain misbehavior is suppressed and another one is substituted for it. After biting Louis's thigh, Lorraine is helped to restore her feminine dignity with an apology. Don restates in acceptable language the offensive statements he had impulsively shouted at a classmate. In both of the above instances, the teacher would reward the substitute responses by approving Lorraine's courtesy and Don's acceptable language, carefully pointing out that an individual is more apt to obtain what he wants from others through personal consideration instead of through abusive attack. The reader will once again observe the general strategy of rewarding acceptable social behaviors that are incompatible with deviant behaviors. Also bear in mind that the effective use of restitution requires that the student have a suitable social response to substitute for the misbehavior.

Another factor that affects the permanence of punishment procedures centers around the timing of negative sanctions. Available evidence indicates rather consistently that children who are punished early in a given sequence of misbehavior develop greater resistance to temptation than those who are punished only after completion of the misdeed. Moreover, the longer the punishment is withheld while the child is in the process of misbehaving, the weaker the subsequent behavioral suppression. What are the implications for classroom practice? Specifically, the teacher should punish before the misbehavior is in full force. This arrangement, as teachers will tell you, is not always possible. Sometimes the situation just explodes without much warning. Although classroom explosions of the spontaneous combustion variety do occur, it is nonetheless frequently possible to spot the trouble coming. According to accounts given by many teachers, they are able to observe, for instance, a chain of behavior leading to classroom fights or other uncontrolled outbursts. A not unfamiliar aggressive sequence is as follows: a disagreement over some trivial matter, threatening behavior, making unkind remarks about one another, pushing or shoving behavior, and finally actual fighting. If a "time-out" period is selected as the punishment of choice, then it should be applied at the time of "disagreement" or "threatening behavior."

Teachers can also spot other behaviors that lead to difficulty such as cheating on classroom examinations, continuous whistling or desk shoving, and pilfering from other students' desks. In these particular instances a knowing glance or a quiet but firm reminder of the rule may constitute sufficient early punishment.

Early punishment most likely serves to attach fear to the behaviors that lead up to the serious violations of classroom rules. Once a misbehavior is well underway, however, rewards from a self-rewarding behavior or the peer group probably serve to maintain and facilitate the undesirable behavior and, thus, to some extent, override (counteract or nullify) the inhibitory effects of punishment. If you punish late in the chain of events, the student has probably already accomplished to a great extent what he set out to do, that his behavior has paid off for him. Moreover, it might well be that the teacher who uses early punishment is perceived by the students as strict and, for this reason too, they refrain from further violations (Bandura, 1969). Whatever the theoretical explanation, the timing of punishment is apparently related to the child's resistance to deviation. Early punishment also has the advantage of stopping behavior immediately. And as all teachers know, there are occasions when the child's misbehavior cannot be tolerated and must be stopped abruptly. The writer recalls one explosive group of students among whom behaviors such as hitting, shoving, tripping, hairpulling, name calling, and the destruction of other student's property had to be called to a halt very quickly so that this aggressive behavior did not spread throughout the entire class. Despite the presence of a large number of acting-out students, peace and calm prevailed in the classroom under the firm leadership of a veteran teacher. Chaotic conditions arose, however, when a new teacher took over the reins because of his failure to take immediate action once he saw trouble coming. His indecisiveness was costly. Instead of quickly and consistently giving the disorderly student a "time-out" period, as was needed in this particular situation, he would adopt a "wait and see" attitude. As a consequence, there would sometimes be as many as four to five separate fist fights raging at a given time. Punishment is far more effective when its intensity is introduced at full intensity than when it is introduced gradually. A firmly presented time-out period is more effective than several "no's" of increasing loudness.

Lack of Direction

Punishment simply serves notice to stop inappropriate behaviors. It does not indicate to the student what behaviors are appropriate in the situation. How often do we catch ourselves saying things like: "George, stop that and do what you're suppose to be doing." "Sally, quit that fooling around and do it right." "Pete, do you have to do that. Settle down!" "Don, get with it!" Our verbal reprimands make it painfully clear to students that we want them to cease misbehaving but rarely make explicit what we want them to do. Consequently, the student may frequently not know exactly how he is to remedy the situation. Have you ever had somebody yell at you and yet not know specifically what was wanted or how to accomplish it? It can be a bewildering experience, especially if a powerful authority figure is making the demands on you.

By now, we have also answered in part the second limitation associated with the use of punishment as a means of modifying behavior, namely, the problem posed by lack of direction. Because negative sanctions do not tell the student what he should do, it is imperative that we as teachers allow or offer the student acceptable alternative modes of behavior that can then be rewarded. To leave him frustrated, bewildered and, perhaps, stewing as a consequence of enforced negative sanctions is not only unnecessarily harsh but often ineffective. In the case of the whining girl, she should be given an opportunity for gaining her way through socially accepted channels, and rewarded when she does use these channels. She should be rewarded when she learns to say "Please" and when she shows that she can be a good sport (Hunter, 1967). Undesired behavior will be eliminated more quickly by teaching the student alternative behaviors to take the place of the ones suppressed by punishment. The teaching of new responses can be facilitated through the use of modeling procedures (to be discussed in the next section) and of positive reward.

Avoidance Misbehaviors

Foremost among the unfavorable side effects of punishment is the development of avoidance behaviors. It is common knowledge that we have a strong tendency to avoid contact with individuals and situations that we find unpleasant. Apparently, withdrawal from punishing settings is sufficiently rewarding to outweigh the unrewarding consequences brought on by the avoidance behavior. Consider, for example, the classroom setting wherein avoidance behaviors commonly take the form of lying, cheating, sneakiness, class skipping, becoming sick, hiding, withdrawing, doodling, humming, and the like. Such escape behaviors are rewarding to the student in that they remove temporarily, at least, the punishment. Cheating can get rid of low grades, truancy removes the student from an unpleasant teacher and school curriculum, daydreaming takes away the dislike associated with reading, and lying shuts off the feared consequences of telling the truth. In many instances, these resulting escape behaviors may be more unwholesome than the behavior that the original punishment was designed to eliminate. Moreover, once these escape behaviors become established, they can be difficult to eliminate.

One especially unfortunate consequence of escape behaviors is an avoidance of teachers and/or other change agents. As Bandura (1969) notes, this can prove a particularly serious hindrance in that it deprives the student of the opportunity to learn both attitudes and behaviors normally acquired through unforced modeling. "With restricted social contact, there can be little identificatory learning" (Bandura, 1969).

Many psychologists today recognize two "types" of punishment. Basically, negative consequences can involve the presentation of painful experiences or the removal of rewards. In the school setting, punishments falling in the latter category may take the form of time-out procedures, exclusion and loss of privileges. Punishments in the former category include physical punishment (ear pulling, arm squeezing, pushing, slapping, or restraining) verbal reprimands (yelling, scolding, raising one's voice, threats, sarcasm), facial expressions (frowning, grimacing, head shaking, "evil eye," "dirty looks"), and extra assignments (for example, write one hundred times, "I will not. . . ."). Although both are forms of punishment, they produce somewhat different side effects and reactions toward teachers. Notice, for instance, that not all forms of punishment produce avoidance behaviors. Instead, such fear learning is most likely to accompany situations in which punishment involves the presentation of punitive stimuli. On the other hand, when the withdrawal of rewards is used by warm parents, children seem to develop self-control and social conscience. In brief, by a careful selection of punishment procedures, the teacher can drastically reduce or prevent the unfortunate consequences of emotional conditioning that lead to avoidance behaviors.

Specificity of punishment also helps to safeguard the teacher-pupil relationship since, by punishing specific undesirable behaviors and by rewarding acceptable behavior, the student is helped to understand that we only disapprove of certain of his negative acts and that we do not reject him as a person. Thus, instead of saying, "Don, can't you ever behave," or "Louise, do you always have to make a pest of yourself," it would be better to say, "Don, I think you could work better if you turned around the right way in your seat," or "Louise, throwing books is not allowed."

Behavioral Constriction

In this section we are concerned with two other consequences that can stem from the use of punishment; namely, the inhibition of socially desirable behaviors and the development of personal rigidity. The effects of punishment are not always confined to the behaviors that we want eliminated. Harsh punishments, especially those applied over lengthy periods of time, can also lead to the inhibition of socially desirable behaviors and to a loss of spontaneity. In other words, the punished student may come to suppress socially acceptable patterns of behavior that are not in need of censor. Take, for instance, the prolonged and severe punishment of aggressive behavior. Now, a certain amount of aggression is a sign of a robust and well-balanced personality. As such, socialization processes both at home and school must not be so repeatedly harsh as to suppress appreciably aggressive behaviors. Although punitive disciplinary practices may well eventually eliminate troublesome aggressive acts, they may also stifle assertiveness and competitiveness, thereby placing the student at a distinct disadvantage in later life in that training in aggression is necessary not only for the fulfillment of the male's economic role but for other aspects of psychosocial functioning as well.

As a consequence of this generalization to other aspects of behavior, the student may also become less flexible in his adjustment. Repeated severe punishment, for example, has been found to increase the child's anxiety about aggressive thoughts, feelings, and acts. This aggression anxiety can lead the student to feel uncomfortable and apprehensive in situations where aggressive impulses, his own as well as others, are aroused or where hostile acts are carried out. In settings of this nature, the student may commonly respond with feelings of fear, guilt, embarrassment, or self-deprecation. In brief, the student has become less flexible in his response to situations that involve aggression. His behavioral freedom or adaptability has, in a very genuine sense, become lessened. He may even go so far as to avoid numerous situations that arouse his anxiety over aggression, leading to further personality constriction.

To guard against behavioral constriction, the teacher should reward acceptable behaviors that are related or similar in nature to the ones being punished. For instance, hitting others may be punished but desirable assertiveness may be rewarded. Thus, the student may be punished for physically assaultive behavior in conjunction with playground play but praised for appropriately assertive behavior in a football game, in a spelling bee, or in his role as stage manager for a forthcoming play. Similarly, a student may be punished for playing in math class when he should be working. Yet, he should be encouraged (rewarded) to engage in play at recess and at appropriate times in the classroom. It is certainly not our intention as teachers to produce people who cannot enjoy life, especially at times when to do so is both natural and healthy. This sort of selective reinforcement greatly assists the student to discriminate what behaviors are acceptable for a given situation. Discrimination learning is also greatly enhanced if the teacher clearly labels the modes of behavior that are acceptable and those that are punishable. Moreover, in spelling out these rules or verbal guidelines, the teacher should specify the times and places at which certain behaviors are deemed suitable or unsuitable. Under such clear-cut arrangements, greater specificity of punishment can be ensured. The punishment of specific behaviors is desirable in that it has been shown to have informative and beneficial effects. In brief, punishment when it is used in conjunction with discrimination training need not impair the student's flexible responsiveness.

Undesirable Modeling

On many occasions, the teacher's words or direct teachings say one thing to the student while his actions or indirect teachings say something contradictory. Parents, for example, who use power-assertive techniques to control aggression tend to produce children who behave in an aggressive fashion toward their peers. Unwittingly, parents and teachers provide a clear-cut model of the very kind of behavior from which they want their children or students to refrain. What the child appears to learn is that aggression should not be directed toward those more powerful but that it is permissible to aggress toward those of equal or lesser power. Harsh punishment is also apt to function as an additional source of frustration which, in turn, may facilitate further hostile feelings and acts.

How do we guard against the effects of negative modeling? Since indirect teaching may counteract the effects of direct teachings, it is evident that teachers and other social agents, for that matter, should refrain from modeling punitive forms of behavior. Negative modeling, in addition to possibly nullifying the effects of direct training, may also increase the likelihood that, through imitation, the student on future occasions will display the teacher's undesirable behavior. Hence, teachers who verbally espouse a democratic philosophy but who react in a rigid, restrictive, and punitive authoritarian way in their handling of stressful class situations undoubtedly curtail the impact of their intentional instruction and increase the probability that their students will respond similarly in comparable situations. The negative modeling influence is especially apt to occur when punishment entails the presentation of painful consequences to the student. On the other hand, punishment that entails the removal of rewards seemingly minimizes the unfortunate result of undesirable modeling. More will be said of modeling procedures later in the text (see table 5.1).

TABLE 5.1

Punishment: A Summary of Problems and Solutions

Undesirable Side Effects and Limitations	Ways to Prevent or Minimize
1. Transitory suppressive effects	1. Combine punishment and reward
2. Does not indicate what is appropriate behavior	2. Provide and reward acceptable alternative behaviors
3. Produces avoidance behaviors	3. Use removal of rewards as a form of punishment; use behavioral contracts
4. Reduces behavioral flexibility	4. Combine punishment and discrimination learning procedures
5. Teacher becomes undesirable model	5. Avoid modeling punitive forms of behavior

TWO FORMS OF PUNISHMENT

Despite the widespread and almost daily use of punishment in the classroom, there has been very little in the way of systematic study on the effects of this technique as a means of changing student behavior.

Because there are two "kinds" of punishment[1]—the inflicting of pain versus the removal of reinforcers—that vary in their effectiveness and in their side effects, they will be discussed separately.

Inflicting Pain

Frequency of Teacher Criticism. Even the best teacher on occasion will resort to this form of punishment in an effort to secure desired behavior. As mentioned earlier, this form of punishment manifests itself in such teacher activities as threats, sarcasm, dirty looks, shaking, and the like.

Some of the recent work in this area has been done by Wesley Becker and his associates at the University of Illinois. In one of their studies, they investigated the effects of frequency of teacher criticism (Thomas, Becker, and Armstrong, 1968). A class of 28 well-behaved middle elementary students was chosen for study. In one phase of the experiment, the effects of teacher behavior on classroom behaviors were investigated

---

[1] The distinction between these two forms of punishment is not always hard and fast. A spanking, for example, by a teacher or parent with whom the child has a warm relationship might well be construed as the withdrawal of love. That is, what ordinarily would be objectively perceived as the inflicting of pain could, in the child's eyes, be tantamount to the removal of a reward. It is probably more accurate to conceive of these forms of punishment as existing along a continuum rather than as being dichotomous. Thus we really do not have clear-cut types of punishment. Instead, it is a matter of which we will emphasize.

by varying the number of disapproving transactions that the teacher had with her students. Disapproving teacher behaviors fell into three categories—physical contact, for example, grabbing a student, verbal contacts, for example, "If you don't settle down, then you can stay after," and facial expressions, for example grimacing. In one particular phase of the study, the teacher tripled the number of critical interactions with her students with the result that disruptive behavior now occurred in more than 31 percent of the time period observed as compared to an 8.7 percent incidence figure under normal classroom conditions. Of the various disruptive behaviors studied, noisemaking (crumpling paper, tapping feet, throwing objects, etc.), gross motor activities (getting out of seat, rocking, skipping, arm flailing, etc.), and orienting misbehavior (turning one's head or body toward another student, looking at others, and showing things to others) all increased. Only verbalizations (talking to others, laughing, whistling, coughing, etc.) declined when the teacher increased the number of critical comments that she made to her students. This latter finding is in all probability an artifact of the scoring system in that observers could not score a behavior as a verbalization unless they could hear the child's responses. Actually, student talk did increase; however, the students talked quietly to avoid being caught by the teacher. Lip movements and head turning did increase, but the verbalizations could not be heard. Why did disruptive behavior increase? Nobody can be sure in a complex field study like this, since simultaneous control of all relevant factors cannot be achieved. The investigators did advance two hypotheses to explain the increase in misbehavior. First, peer support of misbehavior occurs when the teacher makes a high number of critical comments. This would suggest that unless the teacher supports acceptable behavior with suitable consequences, student behavior will be controlled by the peer group in ways that are apt to be at odds with the teacher's objectives. Second, there is the possibility that critical comments may actually increase some misbehaviors. Recall the study discussed earlier on sit-down behaviors. The more first graders were told to sit down, the more they were out of their seats.

Intensity of Teacher Criticism. Much remains to be learned about the effects of intense punishment on misbehavior. One reason for our state of advanced ignorance is that we do not always know what constitutes intense punishment for a given individual. For example, a sensitive student might be crushed when relieved of a classroom responsibility that afforded him status, for example, feeding the class pet. On the other hand, we all know certain students who are almost totally unresponsive to teacher shouting or even paddlings. Teachers also realize that the effects of intense punishment are highly dependent on factors such as timing (early versus late punishment), frequency, and consistency. Despite the gaps and inconsistencies in this area, it appears that high-intensity punishments are required to suppress behavior under certain conditions—when punishment is used occasionally as opposed to frequently, when the misbehavior is firmly entrenched, when the misbehavior is still highly rewarded, and when the student does not have suitable alternative behaviors that teachers can reward (Bandura, 1969).

One study, again conducted by Becker and his associates, had to do with the intensity of punishment, a topic rarely studied in the classroom (O'Leary and Becker, 1969). This study involved a first grade class of 19 children during their rest period and it consisted of five phases: phase I, a base phase to observe and record behavior under ordinary classroom conditions; phase II in which appropriate behavior was praised and inappropriate behavior ignored; phase III in which disruptive behavior was quietly reprimanded; phase IV in which disruptive behavior was reprimanded in a way audible to the entire class; and phase V in which appropriate behavior was again praised and disruptive behavior ignored. During phase I, there was an average of 54 percent deviant behavior. Observers noticed that praise was used sparingly whereas reprimands were commonly used. During phase II, there was a decrease in deviant behavior to 32 percent. In phase III, the percentage of misbehavior was 39 percent with the teacher averaging 11 reprimands per day and no praise incidents. In phase IV, the deviant behavior increased to 53 percent as the teacher made critical remarks that the whole class could hear. The teacher averaged 14 critical comments per day, and no praise incidents were noted. In phase V, the student misbehavior dropped to a 35 percent figure. Several findings are of interest. First, praising appropriate behavior and ignoring inappropriate behavior again appears as a means for reducing disruptive behavior. More important with respect to our present topic of punishment was the finding that quiet reprimands are about as effective as praise in controlling behavior. Although there is a growing body of evidence to suggest that negative teacher attention may strengthen troublesome behaviors and may increase their rate of frequency, the present findings indicate that the intensity of the critical comments is a significant factor. Loud reprimands increased disruptive behaviors, but quiet reprimands decreased them. As the investigators point out, it makes a great difference whether a teacher calmly and matter of factly asks a student to rest his head on the desk or whether she shouts at him to put his head down. Whereas loud reprimands increase the likelihood that other students will pay attention to the misbehaving student, quiet reprimands preclude peer group reward. The main conclusion of this study is that we should praise acceptable behaviors and should use calm but firm reprimands for misbehavior. As noted earlier, the combination of reward and punishment can be an effective means of reducing inappropriate behavior. The most ineffective classroom manager is probably one who reprimands frequently and in a loud manner.

The results of these studies are consistent with the earlier findings of Anderson and Brewer (1946) who observed that dominating teachers who used force, threats, shame, and blame affected children's adjustments adversely. Children working under these conditions generally displayed nonconforming behavior. Personal hostility in the classroom does not appear to be a productive force. However, impersonal punishment of an intense nature may yield beneficial results, as we shall see in the section on systematic exclusion.

Negative Practice. This technique, although not widely practiced, is nevertheless one that is not unfamiliar to teachers. The basic rationale is to have the student repeat an uncontrolled, involuntary behavior to the point that it assumes an aversive association. For example, a nail-biter would be asked to bite his nails for a period of time sufficient to insure that nail-biting—once a pleasurable activity—now becomes unpleasant and something to be avoided. Or a boy who loses frequent control of himself might be asked to have temper tantrums well beyond the point at which they cease to be satisfying to him. This technique increases the child's awareness of behaviors that, because of their frequency, have become automatic or habitual. In other words, the punishment associated with the given behavior serves as a signal or cue that alerts him to stop the involuntary acts. For example, when the nailbiter, following negative practice sessions, starts to raise his hand to his mouth, he becomes conscious of what he is doing. As you recall, punishment helps one to remember what not to do.

There are two basic ingredients required for the successful use of this method—the individual must be motivated to change his behavior, and the behavior in question must be repeated until it becomes punishing, since stopping the repetitions halfway would only strengthen the maladaptive behavior (Woody, 1969). As implied above, negative practice is used to modify involuntary, compulsive behaviors such as thumb-sucking, tics, hair-pulling, scratching, nose-picking, and stuttering. This technique has yet to be subjected to extensive clinical and research experimentation. Consequently, evaluation would be premature at this point. As Woody (1969) notes, however, negative practice does fit well into the framework of dealing with children. If validated, this approach would offer another means that teachers could use in managing certain kinds of bothersome behaviors.

Removal of Rewards: Toward a More Positive Use of Punishment

The removal of rewards is a technique widely used by teachers to encourage students to forego undesirable behavior. The removal of rewards differs from extinction in that the latter simply involves discontinuing the reward that ordinarily follows a given misbehavior, whereas in the former punishing consequences are applied through the loss of privileges. Consider the case of an acting-out child whose behavior is maintained by peer approval. If the teacher decided to use extinction procedures as a means of weakening this misbehavior, he would simply ignore the child's assaultive tactics and would entice the peer group to do likewise. Thus, the reward that maintains the behavior would then have been removed. Suppose, however, that the teacher could not remove the reward (peer approval) which is maintaining the misbehavior. In this event, he would then pit the loss of privileges, for example, removing recess against the reward of peer approval. The effectiveness of this form of punishment will depend, in part, on how much the student values the respective rewards (peer approval versus recess). As pointed out earlier, this procedure typically involves the loss of privileges. While the removal of rewards is effective, it can also be overdone. Thus, for example, the teacher should not remove privileges for extended periods of time just to impress on the student the seriousness of his misbehavior. For if unpleasantness is dragged out too long, the punishment seems arbitrary and unnecessarily unpleasant. If privileges are taken away, we must be sure to specify ways to regain them.

Examples of rewards to be withheld until the student complies with the teacher's requests or until he makes restitutions are presented in Table 5.2.

In this section, we discuss two variations of this approach, one of which is generally used (the time-out procedure) and one which although apparently effective, is not as widely used as it might be (systematic exclusion).

Time-out Procedures.   One punishment frequently enforced by teachers involves isolation from the group. Hall (1966) has reported on this procedure with respect to its use with a group of unmanageable boys. The teacher established the principle of mutual respect which stated that the teacher is there to teach, the student is there to learn, and that these

TABLE 5.2

Rewards To Be Withheld

Cannot sit next to friend or in seat of own choice.

Cannot attend pep rally or any planned school activity (also field trips).

Loss of phonograph and tape recorder privileges (or loss of use of any classroom game or equipment).

Shortened recess, lunch period, or no early dismissal.

Loss of prestige or recognition symbol—first in line, going on errands, being monitor, being librarian for the day, being a patrol guard, caretaker of class pet.

Shortening classroom activities enjoyed by class (physical education, art, music).

Confiscating toy for prescribed length of time.

Revoking special passes or limiting access to drinking fountain, gum chewing, or pencil sharpening when privilege is abused.

Unable to visit other classes (to be reader's aid or interested in subject area).

Loss of tangible reward, for example, toys, passes, magazines for a given length of time, or until behavior improves.

Unable to have special discussion groups or panel activities on current topics because of misuse of time in class.

Loss of free time or free-time group activity (talent show, playing popular records).

Dropped from club membership until behavior improves.

Unable to participate in some planned group activity, for example, tug-of-war, snow fight, and the like.

Little or no feedback comments on papers (no smiling Sam or current sayings).

Delay of showing films.

Not letting the child pick a choice from the reinforcement menu.

rights were not to be infringed on. The teacher was not to shame, belittle, or downgrade the student. On the other hand, the student was not to violate the rights of the teacher to teach nor of his classmates to learn. In brief, both teacher and students were to regard each other as worthy of attention, concern, and respect. When an infringement occurred, the teacher simply pointed to the violator, and he removed himself without any conversation about the incident. The student could return when he felt he was ready, that is, when he could respect the rights of others. It took several months for this process to take effect, and it was assisted through the use of a special curriculum that was of high interest to the boys; but the technique did accomplish its purpose without the usual negative attitudes that accompany punishment.

If a teacher is to use time-out procedures effectively, he must be sure that removal from the class is a punishment. If removal from the group is rewarding instead of punishing, then it will not be effective in modifying the student's misbehavior. If the student is able to talk with friends who pass by in the hall or to look at his friends in the classroom and

laugh, then the time-out becomes a rewarding experience and his misbehavior pays off for him. Ideally, the students should be placed in a
dull, unstimulating room containing a chair and a light. Many teachers
complain that they cannot use this technique, since they have no special
isolation rooms. Actually, a special room is not always necessary. Many
teachers have used screens effectively to isolate students. The screen is
placed at the back of the room in a position such that the student is
out of the sight of his peers but in the sight of his teacher. Other teachers
who did not have screens have isolated the disruptive student by seating
him between the wall and the filing cabinet.

In enforcing the time-out procedure, the teacher should be firm but
matter of fact, as though the child experienced a logical or natural consequence for his misbehavior.[2] The teacher must guard against the tendency to yell and scold at this time, since this often has a tendency to
strengthen unacceptable behavior through teacher attention. The troublemaker is to leave without fanfare. Extended discussion or "reasoning"
at this time is contraindicated since the teacher attention probably
strengthens the undesired behavior. The probabilities of achieving a
quiet dismissal are substantially enhanced if the consequences of misbehavior have been previously agreed on by the teacher and student.
More will be said regarding this matter when the use of behavioral contracts is discussed. Finally, the teacher must be consistent and must
isolate the student immediately every time he breaks the rule in question.

A variation of this technique seems to work well with the passively
resistant child who, although not upsetting to the class, will not do his
work. Children of this sort typically resist authority by bringing the
wrong book to class, by forgetting an assignment at home, by losing the
place when reciting, or by interrupting schoolwork to sharpen a pencil
or to empty a bladder. Keirsey (1965) refers to his approach as the "two
seat method." In this method, the child has one seat when he is a part
of the class and works with other students, and a second seat when he is
not a part of the class and is not receiving instruction. The student selects which of his two seats he wants to sit in, and this cues the teacher
that he does or does not want to work with the group. The success of
this approach with passive resistive students probably stems in large measure from a reduction of the "you-versus-me" element in teacher pupil
relationships. Under this regimen, it is the student who administers punishment to himself.

----

[2] It is a good idea to give one (but only one) warning prior to isolation in the
hope that the warning itself will be sufficiently punishing so as to eliminate the need
for the time-out procedure.

Systematic Exclusion and Behavior Contracts. Systematic exclusion, which has been widely used in the elementary schools of California since 1957, is an extension of the time-out technique. The main difference between the two is that under a program of systematic exclusion the student is sent home instead of being isolated in the school. It is estimated that about one in every 500 students will need this type of approach (Keirsey, 1969). The basic rationale is "to confront the child with the immediacy, naturalness, predictability, and impersonality of the consequences of his behavior. Whatever he does, he does to himself. The teacher, principal, counselor, and parent abstain from lecturing, scolding, or punishing, or even discussing his behavior. The responsibility for managing himself rests with the child" (Kaplan, 1970).

Systematic exclusion or suspension therapy, as it is sometimes called, frequently entails the use of a behavior contract, which is an agreement between two or more persons specifying what each will do for a stated time period (Krumboltz and Thoresen, 1969). The idea is that "I'll do this for you, if you'll do that for me." Two purposes of the contract are to teach the chronically misbehaving student that privileges entail responsibilities and to make him use his own resources for control.

A good contract must meet five requirements (Dinoff and Rickard, 1969). The first requirement is that all rules must be described explicitly. Second, the contract must be fair to both parties so that neither feels taken advantage of. Third, the goals of the contract must be mutually agreed on. Fourth, the contract must make reasonable and feasible demands. Last, the contract should end on a note of mutual satisfaction, thus laying the groundwork for future behavioral contracts in other areas, if needed. Contracts differ from rules in that the latter are typically applied to the student when he had no voice in structuring them. With contracts, each party plays a direct part in determining the rewards and punishments with certain clearly specified rules. If he abuses the privilege of going to school through a rule infraction, his freedom to attend school is restricted. (See pages 122–123 for an example of one behavioral contract.) Many educators, on first hearing of this approach to changing behavior, argue that staying in school is not rewarding for most disorderly students. Research studies indicate, however, that for the elementary school pupil, at least, school is rewarding and that removal of this reward is effective in producing acceptable school behavior. Clinical experience also strongly suggests that school, somewhat surprisingly at first glance, is the most enjoyable part of the day for many maladjusted elementary school children.

According to one survey, teachers and pupils apparently view systematic suspension more favorably than do parents. Of the 22 teachers who at that time had students under systematic suspension, all reported improvements in their pupils' behavior. Moreover, 95 percent of the pupils felt that they were better behaved. Only 63 percent of the parents, however, took a positive view of the process. Moreover, it was difficult for parents to play their role as objective, nonpunitive bystanders, and when they did, they did not like it. It is understandable that parents would have trouble in assuming this role. As far as the children were concerned, none of their parents had lived up to their agreement to do or to say nothing when the child was sent home. Yet, systematic suspension worked successfully with the large majority of youngsters. These students were better accepted by their classmates, they liked school better, and their schoolwork improved. It is interesting to observe that 100 percent of the teachers in this study were willing to recommend this technique for use with other students. Keirsey (1969) notes that this technique, which has been used on hundreds of children for almost two decades works in 75 percent to 90 percent of the cases. Brown and Shields (1967) state that in their experience only two children out of approximately 200 did not respond favorably to some degree to this technique. Both of these students preferred to stay at home to annoy their mothers rather than to remain in school with their class.

This approach will not work with every troublesome student. As with the time-out procedure, it is important to select for systematic exclusion those youngsters who want to go to school and to remain with the group. It is for this reason, perhaps, that this technique has been most widely used with youngsters below the seventh grade level (Lyons and Powers, 1963). There has been little, if any, research on its use with older age groups. One cannot necessarily take the child's word with respect to his liking for school, since many students who have responded well to suspension therapy have denied the importance of school for them. Both psychological study and teacher judgment are probably more useful ways of determining how motivated the child is to be a group member. Experience indicates that this approach achieves less favorable results with school phobic and overprotected children who prefer to remain at home with their mothers, with the extremely aggressive antisocial child (the psychopathic child) who has difficulty in identifying with his peers and teachers, and last with the "martyr" who likes to overdramatize situations such as the planning conferences attended by parents and school personnel as part of his exclusion from school. In the latter case, the systematic exclusion program plays right into his hand, allowing him to go "on stage" as a martyr (Keirsey, 1969). Suspension therapy can be pursued with the "martyr" if the program is instituted directly without fanfare.

Exclusion for this child must be automatic so that he is not rewarded for his histrionics.

Happily, the number of disruptive children discussed above are relatively rare. The youngster who frequently causes teachers the most upset is not the one who has an occasional acute outburst but, instead, is the student who displays chronic misbehavior. Each misdeed may in and of itself seem trivial, but the cumulative buildup becomes devastating. That is, it is not so much what this student does as how frequently he does it. The constant bumping, snickering, desk moving, talking, loud yawning, pencil sharpening, strange noises, and wandering are the kind of annoyances that get to a teacher and impair his efficiency. Systematic exclusion works well with students "mainly of the acting-out impulsive type who enjoy and demand release of their feelings but do not associate this kind of behavior with consequences, whose parents have not taught them the concept of consequences, have not followed through with them or have allowed themselves to be manipulated by their children" (Brown and Shields, 1967). This technique has also worked well with the mentally retarded and with the brain-injured, although this system reportedly must be applied over a longer period of time with this latter group.

EXAMPLES OF PUNISHMENT

Problem: The use of foul language in class

Punishment: Inflicting pain

The problem in this particular high school class concerned the habitual use of abusive language. The more bad words the student used, the higher his status in the peer group. It was clearly a case whereby peer group values conflicted with values of the school. Realizing that the peer rewards had to be broken down or changed, the teacher enlisted student support in developing a class code. One of the rules that was mutually agreed on called for the use of proper language in the classroom. This rule was to be enforced by assessing a fine of fifteen cents per violation. Since the fines were to be spent on suitable activities that the entire class enjoyed (sports events, class picnics, special field trips), the peer group did an outstanding job of policing foul language.

Comment. Notice that the use of punishment to cope with a frequent misbehavior, the importance of involving the peer group in the formation of rules, and the use of presenting painful stimulation, namely, fines, as a sanction to back up the rule. It is especially interesting to observe that the teacher by sharing his authority actually strengthened his position.

•   •   •

Problem: Constant nose-picking

Punishment: Negative practice

Tom was constantly picking his nose, much to the disgust of his teacher and his classmates. Tom had picked his nose so often that this behavior became habitual to the point that he seemed unaware of this behavior. The teacher decided to do something about this situation. She called Tom aside one day and asked him if he was aware of how frequently he picked his nose and how it might look to others? Tom replied that he really had not thought much about it. At this point, the teacher gave Tom a mirror and asked him to look at himself while he picked. He acknowledged the fact that such behavior was unbecoming and that he would try to refrain from this activity. The teacher said that she might be able to help him suppress the nose-picking. Tom was to pick his nose in private before school started, at recess time, and after school. Each nose-picking session lasted ten minutes and the teacher would usually pair the picking with disapproving comments, for example, "See how ugly that looks." The teacher also said that she would assist him in class by giving him a signal (gently stroking the side of her nose) whenever she noticed him inadvertently engaging in nose-picking. The nose-picking sessions were no longer needed after a week but the signal continued to be used. Under this regimen, the frequency of this irritating and objectionable behavior diminished rapidly.

Comment. This case illustrates the informational or cue value of negative practice in dealing with involuntary behaviors. That is, it helped Tom to become more aware of raising his hand to his nose and picking. Whereas hand-raising and picking previously were pleasurable, these activities quickly assumed unpleasant connotations.

·   ·   ·

Problem: Messy classroom

Punishment: Removal of a reward

One sixth grade teacher was quite disgusted with the way students left their things strewn around the classroom. Despite repeated reprimands and (unfulfilled) threats, the classroom looked like a mess. On the advice of the school psychologist, she told the class that this messing was upsetting to her. She then announced that starting with the next day she was bringing in a storage box and that anything left lying about would be put in this locked box. Moreover, the claimed articles would have to stay in the box for a period of five class days. On the positive side, the teacher decided to offer greater incentive for neatness and orderliness by allowing students who displayed those attributes to select rewards from an attractive reinforcement menu.

Comment. This case illustrates the effective use of withholding rewards and of combining punishment with reward. Again we see punishment being used to control misbehavior when it is frequent.

. . .

Problem: Physical aggression
Punishment: Multiple techniques

Dave was the strongest boy in his seventh grade class and enjoyed intimidating others with his physical superiority. In gym class, he would threaten to drown or dunk fellow students. On the playground, he would challenge others to fight with him. Because of his aggressive tactics, other students would sometimes cry hysterically and refuse to go to gym or out for recess. The teacher told Dave that he would be isolated everytime he threatened a classmate (that is, removed from gym or recess). The students were told to "pretend Dave doesn't exist" when they were challenged by him. If ignoring did not work on those occasions, they were then to shame him by saying in a nonbelligerent but firm way, "It wouldn't prove anything if you did beat me up, because you're so much bigger than I am. Why don't you pick on somebody who is your own size." To insure the continued use of appropriate assertive behavior, Dave was rewarded for his ability to move big boxes and tables around the classroom, his displays of strength in tug-of-war matches, and by assigning him the responsibility of enforcing the newly promulgated class rule that bigger students are not to pick on smaller students. Through patient and constant application of this program, Dave gradually learned over the course of the school year when and where the use of his physical superiority was called for and uncalled for.

Comment. The successful resolution of this case involved the combined use of several techniques—removal of rewards (time-out periods), inflicting pain (shame from peer group), and discrimination learning (rewarding assertive behavior in appropriate times and places).

. . .

Problem: Hostile-destructive behavior
Punishment: Early punishment (time-out procedure)

Bill is a bright ten-year-old deaf student whose hostile and destructive behavior frequently disrupts the class. On numerous occasions he loses complete control of himself. In analyzing his outbursts, the teacher detected the following chain of events.

1. Bill experiences frustration, often times because of his inability to express himself well orally. His thoughts seem to far outdistance his speech.
2. He has negative responses to every assignment.
3. He rolls a pencil back and forth on the desk top.
4. He rocks his chair in a violent manner.
5. He laughs out loud.
6. He makes obscene gestures toward others.
7. He gets out of his seat to hit others and throw things.
8. He threatens the teacher with physical abuse—sometimes he hits others.
9. He loses complete control and goes wildly around the room, kicking, screaming, and cursing.

Bill is sometimes able to stop after step three, but the teacher has learned through bitter experience that there is no turning back for Bill once he reaches step four and that she had best give him a "time-out" period at that time. In view of Bill's severe problems, it will probably be necessary to continue using isolation procedures for some time to come. Fortunately, Bill does have some praiseworthy attributes, for example, high intelligence and a strong desire to tutor other deaf students, which the teacher can use to good advantage.

Comment. This study exemplifies the importance of timing in applying punishment procedures. In this case, it was imperative that the teacher did not wait too long before taking action.

•   •   •

Problem: Chronic misbehavior

Punishment: Systematic exclusion

J.F. a third grade male student was constantly talking, out of his seat, and laughing in a strange, high pitch at inappropriate times. When seated, he frequently rocked, chewed on any available object, and made facial grimaces. He often called other students names and enjoyed punching them, especially in the genital area. During one 40-minute sample of his classroom behavior, he was out of his seat five times, made disruptive noises four times, talked fifteen times, and laughed five times. In view of his inability to concentrate, it was not surprising to find that he had difficulty in every academic subject. In brief, J.F. was quite confused, could not follow directions, had extremely poor peer relations, and had trouble with his schoolwork.

As for background information, J.F. was the adopted son of upper middle class parents. The other adopted son in the family was described as a "model" child. J.F. earned a Full Scale IQ of 72 on the Wechsler Intelligence Scale for Children with his Verbal IQ exceeding his Performance IQ by eight points.

During the second parent conference with the principal, teacher, and psychologist in attendance, details of the systematic exclusion program were presented. The following day, another conference was held, which J.F. also attended. After a few opening remarks about how interested everyone there was in J.F., the psychologist told him in a friendly but firm manner that they had made three rules for him and that they were to be followed whenever he was in class. First, no talking. This meant no talking out in class, no talking with neighbors, and no making of strange noises. He was then asked if he knew how to get permission to say something. J.F. stated that he should raise his hand when he wanted to talk. It was clear that he knew what this rule meant. Second, no moving out of your seat without permission. This rule also specified that he was not to move his desk outside of a line on the floor around his desk. He was asked if he had any questions about this rule and if he understood it. Again, the point was made that he could get permission by raising his hand. The third rule was no throwing of anything. This meant no throwing of any object, no snapping of rubber bands, and no blowing through straws. He was then told that each time he disobeyed these rules that his teacher would give him a slip that read, "To the office: Call Mrs. F. and tell her that J.F. is on his way home." There was also space on this sheet for the teacher to initial the rule that J.F. had violated. If asked to leave, he was out for the rest of that day. Furthermore, he was to remain in the house until the time he usually got home from school. He could come back to school the next day and start fresh. Bygones would be bygones. At this time, he was again asked the three rules and told that he would be sent home if he forgot them. The psychologist then said: "We all hope you remember the rules. This is up to you. We can't remember them for you. We can only help you remember them. It's up to you, J.F. Do you understand?"

An analysis of his dismissal pattern over the next five months showed that he was sent home 26 times between November 16 and April 7, that he was sent home most frequently for breaking the talking rule, that he had no favorite days of the week for misbehavior, that one half of his exclusions come within 10 minutes of break bell or 10 minutes after recess or lunch, and that if he was sent home one day he was likely to be sent home the next day as well (20 of his 26 exclusions occurred on two consecutive days). At first he was dejected when he was sent home and expressed an eagerness to stay in school. Later, when his attitude shifted to a "I don't care" stance, school authorities asked the parents to reward J.F. for his full days at school. J.F.'s classroom behavior gradually improved to the extent that he was able to remain in school for the 47 days left in the school year. His behavior outside the classroom did not improve, however. But then again, this was not a part of the program. Without the program of systematic exclusion, his behavior at the start of the next school year was again disruptive. School authorities again considered the resumption of this program (Shier, 1969).

Comment. In brief, systematic exclusion did modify the behavior of this severely disturbed boy for a five-month period. It appears, however, that he will need the continued assistance of this program if he is to remain in school.

Educational Contract*

PARTICIPANTS _____Pupil

_____Teacher

_____Principal

_____Guardian

_____Guardian

_____Attendance
Officer

_____Witness

LIMITS   On violation of any stated limit, the pupil is under suspension from School for _____ day(s).

Aggression: _____
_____

Destruction: _____
_____

Disruption: _____
_____

ROLES   Each signatory agrees to play the role specified, as follows:

TEACHER   On detection of limit violation the teacher will signal the pupil to leave the class. He will on no occasion try to influence the pupil to do or not to do anything (no urging, reminding, coaxing, encouraging, or scolding). He agrees to respect the pupil's *right to fail* or succeed

* From "Systematic Exclusion: Eliminating Chronic Classroom Disruptions" by David W. Keirsey, from *Behavioral Counseling: Cases and Techniques,* edited by John D. Krumboltz and Carl E. Thoresen. Copyright © 1969 by Holt, Rinehart and Winston, Inc. Reprinted by permission of the publisher.

on his own and to acknowledge that he is not responsible for the success or failure of this pupil.

PRINCIPAL On notification or detection of a limit violation the principal will see to it that the pupil leaves the school. He agrees to see to it that the pupil leaves the class when the signal given by the teacher is not acted on by the pupil. When this happens the pupil will be suspended for 3 days including the day of suspension. He agrees to see to it that the parent is notified of the suspension at the earliest possible moment. He agrees that he will not discuss with the pupil in any way the pupil's behavior. (There is to be no persuasion, encouragement, "pep talks," reminders, or scoldings.) He agrees that he is not responsible for the success or failure of this pupil. He agrees to see to it that the attendance officer is notified of all suspensions, absences, and tardinesses, and of the reasons therefore.

PARENT The parents agree that they are not responsible for the success or failure of the pupil at school. They agree that they are fully responsible for the pupil when he is not on school grounds. They absolve the school district of any responsibility whatsoever for this pupil when he is not on school grounds. They agree not to scold or punish the pupil for school behavior or to discuss school behavior with the pupil unless the pupil so desires. They agree that they will not seek explanations for suspensions from any person other than the attendance officer.

ATTENDANCE The attendance officer agrees that he is responsible for supervising
OFFICER breaches of contract and for revising the contract as needed. He agrees to be responsible for processing all absences, suspensions, and tardinesses. He agrees that he is fully responsible for the success or failure of the pupil in school and that he hereby delegates this responsibility to the pupil.

PUPIL The pupil agrees that he is fully responsible for himself and that everything he does and does not do is done or not done *by his own choice.* He agrees to take credit for his failure as well as his success *regardless of how people treat him.*

Dated _____

_____
Pupil

_____
Parent

_____
Parent

_____
Principal

_____
Teacher

_____
Attendance Officer

_____
Witness

•   •   •

Problem: Acting-out behavior of a preschool psychotic boy

Punishment: Combined use of techniques

One team of investigators (Wolf et al., 1964) found a combination of mild punishment and extinction effective in alleviating certain annoying behaviors in a preschool psychotic boy. Among the target behaviors selected for modification were his bedtime difficulties, eating problems, and the throwing of his corrective lenses. His resistance at bedtime was handled by leaving the bedroom door open as long as he would remain in bed. When he got out of bed, however, he was instructed to return to his bed or told that the door would be closed. If he did not comply, the mild aversive consequence, namely, closing the door, was enforced. After the sixth night of this treatment, the boy seldom posed bedtime difficulties during the rest of his stay in the hospital or at home following his discharge. This same boy's eating habits also posed problems for the staff. He used to take food from other children's plates, refused to use silverware, and frequently threw his food around the dining room. These problems were handled by removing his plate for a few minutes whenever he ate with his fingers and by removing the boy himself from the room whenever he snatched food from others or tossed his food about. After a few warnings and his actual removal from the dining room, the boy's food-stealing and food-throwing behaviors were completely eliminated. He also learned to use eating utensils after his plate had been removed several times during one meal. This boy's series of eye operations early in life necessitated the wearing of glasses. His glass-throwing behavior, therefore, obviously had to be controlled, especially since it proved to be moderately expensive. Consequently, Dickie was isolated in a room for 10 minutes following each glass-throwing episode. When a temper tantrum developed in the course of the correction, he had to remain in isolation until it ceased. Within five days, Dickie stopped throwing his glasses. The mother's report is that some six months after Dickie's discharge he is still wearing the glasses, poses no sleeping problems, and engages in no more temper tantrum behavior.

Comment.   By removing the reinforcements for his obnoxious behaviors and by administering mild aversive stimulation, Dickie became a much more manageable and acceptable child. Although still psychotic, Dickie was now a much easier child to live with. Note the counselor's role as a consultant—this time to parents.

•   •   •

Problem: The "naughty finger"

Technique: Removal of a reward

This classroom consisted of 14 mentally retarded students—seven girls and seven boys between the ages of six and ten. A not uncommon gesture that disturbs others is the "naughty finger" (the fist raised with middle finger extended). This gesture not only upsets middle class teachers but disrupts classroom activities as well, since some students return the gesture, others laugh about it, others become angry, and some report this misbehavior to the teacher.

To cope with this problem, the teacher placed ten cards, numbered one to ten, on a bracelet in front of the room and made the following announcement.

> From now on there will be a special 10-minute recess at the end of the day. However, if I see the naughty finger or hear about it, I will flip down one of these cards, and you will have one minute less of recess whenever this happens. Remember, every time I flip down one of these cards, all of you lose a minute from your recess.

The use of this simple tactic reduced this undesirable behavior from an average of 16 occurrences per day to about two (Sulzbacher & Houser, 1968).

Comment. This is a technique that can be easily put to effective use in classrooms whether they consist of mentally retarded children or normal ones. This case also shows that this technique can be employed with groups. In this instance, it promoted group cooperation as well as eliminating a behavior that was disruptive to classroom activities. One variation of this approach would be for the class to establish a rule prohibiting use of the "naughty finger" and then to let the group select a representative to flip down the card when violations occur. In this way, the teacher could assume the role of an interested bystander and not be directly associated with the punishment. Another possibilty might involve some automatic flipping of cards so as to impersonalize the punishment and to make it appear as a natural consequence of one's misbehavior.

SUMMARY

Competent teachers will use rewards more often than punitive measures in managing student behavior. For every punishing experience, there should be approximately four rewarding encounters: yet even the best of teachers will have to use aversive strategies to produce acceptable behavior. Punishment involves a wide variety of practices that the student finds unpleasant. Since punishment is a complex and sometimes unpredictable phenomenon, it must be used as skillfully and carefully as possible. Although its faulty use can produce undesirable side effects, it may well be the method of choice for dealing with troublesome behaviors that are frequent and/or intense. It is rarely desirable to use punishment alone, and it is most effective when presented as a natural consequence of the student's misdeed and when combined with other techniques, especially positive reward. On the positive side, the use of punishment enables the teacher to suppress unacceptable behavior, thereby permitting an opportunity to establish more suitable behaviors through the use of reward. The punishment of specific responses is informative to the student, since it teaches him what he has done wrong. It also has the advantage of stopping behavior immediately and, as every teacher knows, there are occasions when misbehavior must be stopped abruptly. Last, the negative consequences meted out for deviant behavior can serve as a lesson to the rest of the class. Students are less apt to imitate a given misbehavior once they have seen a classmate punished for it and, conversely, students are apt to imitate disruptive behavior if their classmate goes unpunished for his transgression.

A number of factors influence the rate and effectiveness of punishment practices. Among them are factors such as timing, frequency, intensity, and consistency, the nature of the punishment (presentation of painful stimulation versus removal of rewards), the affectional and/or status relationship between the teacher and student and the strength and nature of the behavior being punished (Parke and Walters, 1967).

In conclusion, punishment must have the following characteristics if it is to be used in aiding self-control.

1. It should be related in form to the misbehavior.
2. It must be certain and consistent.
3. It must be fair and just.
4. It must be impersonal.
5. It must be constructive and conducive to better self-control.
6. It should avoid the arousal of fear.
7. It should not involve the assignment of extra work that is unrelated to the act for which the student is being punished. (Sheviakov and Redl, 1944)

REFERENCES

Anderson, H. H., and Brewer, J. E. Studies of teacher's classroom personalities. II. Effects of teachers' dominative and integrative contacts on children's classroom behavior. *Applied Psychological Monographs,* No. 8, 1946.

Ausubel, D. A new look at classroom discipline. *Phi Delta Kappan*, 1961, 43, 25–30.

Bandura, A. *Principles of Behavior Modification*. New York: Holt, Rinehart and Winston, Inc., 1969.

Brown, E. R., and Shields, E. Results of systematic suspension: a guidance technique to help children develop self-control in public school classrooms, *Jour. Special Educ.*, Summer 1967, 1, 425–437.

Dinoff, M., and Rickard, H. C. Learning that privileges entail responsibilities in J. D. Krumboltz and C. E. Thoresen (eds.), *Behavioral Counseling*. New York: Holt, Rinehart and Winston, Inc., 1969, 124–129.

Hall, N. E. The youth development project: A school-based delinquency prevention program, *Jour. School Health*, March 1966, 36, 97–103.

Hunter, M. *Reinforcement*. El Segundo, California: TIP Publications, 1967.

Kaplan, L. *Education and Mental Health*. New York: Harper Row Co., 1970.

Keirsey, D. W. *Transactional Case Work*, Address to Convention of Calif. Assoc. of School Psychologists and Psychometrists, San Francisco, 1965, 23 pp. Mimeo.

Keirsey, D. W. Systematic exclusion: eliminating chronic classroom disruptions in J. D. Krumboltz and C. E. Thoresen (eds.), *Behavioral Counseling*. New York: Holt, Rinehart and Winston, Inc., 1969, 89–114.

Krumboltz, J. D., and Thoresen, C. E., *Behavioral Counseling*. New York: Holt, Rinehart and Winston, Inc., 1969.

Lyons, D. J., and Powers, V. Study of children exempted from Los Angeles schools in N. J. Long, W. C. Morse, and R. G. Newman (eds.), *Conflict in the Classroom: The Education of Emotionally Disturbed Children*, Belmont, Calif.: Wadsworth Publishing Company, 1965, 138–144.

O'Leary, K. D., and Becker, W. C. The effects of the intensity of a teacher's reprimands on children's behavior. *Journal of School Psychology*, 7, 1968–69, 8–11.

Parke, R. D., and Walters, R. H. Some factors influencing the efficacy of punishment training for inducing response inhibition. *Monograph of the Society for Research in Child Development*, 1967, 32, No. 1 (Serial No. 109).

Sheviakov, G., and Redl, F. Discipline yearbook. Department of Supervision and Curriculum, 1944, pp. 7–8.

Shier, D. A. Applying systematic exclusion to a case of bizarre behavior, in J. D. Krumboltz and C. E. Thoresen, *Behavioral Counseling*. New York: Holt, Rinehart and Winston, Inc., 1969, 114–123.

Sulzbacher, S., and Houser, J. A tactic to eliminate disruptive behavior: Group contingent consequences. *American Journal of Mental Deficiency*, 1968, 73, 88–90.

Thomas, D. R., Becker, W. C., and Armstrong, M. Production and elimination of disruptive classroom behavior by systematically varying teacher's behavior, *Journal of Applied Behavior Analysis*, 1, 1968, 35–45.

Wolf, M., Risley, T., and Mees, H. Application of operant conditioning procedures to the behavior problems of an autistic boy. *Behavior Research and Therapy*, 1964, 1, 305–312.

Woody, R. H. *Behavioral Problem Children in the Schools*. New York: Appleton-Century-Crofts, 1969.

6

Overcoming Anxieties Through Desensitization

Desensitization procedures are particularly effective in overcoming intense fears and anxieties.[1] The logic underlying these procedures is simple and straightforward. Identify the events that evoke marked emotional discomfort, arrange the fear producing events into a graded list proceeding from the least to the most disturbing, and associate the unpleasant events with something that elicits intense pleasure. Through repeated association with something pleasant, the feared situation eventually loses its unpleasant connotations. When the individual can relax in the face of what was once an upsetting situation, we say that he has been desensitized. Before examining desensitization procedures further, a few words are in order about the incapacitating effects of intense anxiety on individual functioning.

THE ANXIOUS-WITHDRAWN STUDENT

Teachers, while legitimately concerned with the acting-out student, are also confronted with and often perplexed by the anxious withdrawn child. Although less disruptive to classroom order than his aggressive counterpart, the anxious youngster nonetheless frequently leaves teachers feeling helpless in their efforts to assist him to become more responsive to the classroom setting. The teacher cannot get Jimmy to talk in front of the group, Sally to associate with her classmates, Joe to overcome his

[1] For our purposes, the terms "fear" and "anxiety" are used interchangeably.

128

fear of algebra, Don to conquer his anxiety about tests, Clarence to become more assertive and to defend his rights, or Audrey to stop worrying about making occasional mistakes on assignments. Behaviors like these probably do not interfere with the attainment of educational objectives for the class as a whole, but they do keep the individual thus afflicted from realizing his educational and/or social potential. The plight of anxious-withdrawn child has been aptly described by Morse and Wingo (1969):

> All teachers will have in their classrooms children who are models of conformity yet whose behavior should be considered a problem. There are the unhappy children who have not organized themselves for productive work, the ones who feel grossly inadequate and unimportant, the quiet and withdrawn children, and the shy or fearful ones who often file quietly in and out of school and receive no more than passing consideration. Yet these children are discipline problems as much as the aggresssive, noisy youngster, for they too have not yet learned the mature self-directon that will make their behavior both satisfying to themselves and acceptable to others.

In its more extreme forms, anxiety is most commonly seen in neurotic disorders, for example, the rather total disorganization observed in school phobia. In its less extreme forms the individual feels apprehensive, ill at ease, and that some impending danger is imminent, for example, "I just know something is going to go wrong." Overcompliance to authority, nervous habits, overreaction to criticism, preference for adult company or that of younger children, withdrawal into fantasy as a means of coping with or escape from stressful situations, fear of change in one's daily routines or surroundings, and an inability to face up to stressful conditions are also common manifestations of anxiety.

Current research on anxiety reveals that, when intense, it can have debilitating effects on both intellectual and personality functioning. In terms of intellectual operations, highly anxious students tend to score lower on:

1. Intelligence tests given at both the elementary and secondary school levels.
2. Achievement tests given at both the elementary and secondary school levels.
3. Creativity tests.

In brief, high anxiety appears to affect adversely complex intellectual tasks like the ones that are typically required in the classroom.

Turning to the influence of high anxiety on personality and social functioning, Ruebush (1963) has noted the following.

1. High anxiety pupils when compared to those low in anxiety are not as popular with their peers.

2. High anxiety children are more susceptible to propaganda.

3. High anxiety children have more negative self-concepts and are more self-disparaging. Body image also seems impaired.

4. Dependency is also characteristic of high anxiety children, although more so for boys than for girls.

5. Anxiety decreases the probability of open expression of aggression towards others but increases the probability of these children having feelings of anxiety about aggressive impulses or feelings they experience.

6. Inhibitions and anxiety tend to go hand in hand as manifested behaviorally by indecisiveness, cautiousness, and rigidity.

There are three particular points that we should remember about the anxious, inhibited individual. First, fears are formed very easily by anxious students. That is, fearful responses become more rapidly acquired in the highly anxious person than in his nonanxious counterpart. Second, fear responses are not only readily established in anxiety-provoking situations but they also have a strong tendency to spread to similar situations. Anxiety facilitates generalization. For example, a fear of a particular teacher might well spread to the fear and avoidance of other teachers. A fear of one dog might well generalize to other dogs. A fear learned through association with one exam might make one apprehensive about other exams. A fear of fractions might carry over to other kinds of arithmetic problems yet to be mastered. As Quay (1963) notes, "All of this means that unpleasant and fear-producing experiences are apt to have results quite beyond the immediate setting and such experience should be minimized for this type of child whenever possible."

Finally, once formed, these fear reactions become difficult to extinguish. These avoidance patterns are not learned through reasoning. Thus, when in a similar or identical situation, an emotional response (fear) occurs instead of a rational one. One of the major factors involved in the durability of avoidance behaviors hinges on the fact that the phobic individual does not test his fears against reality anymore. The person who is afraid of dogs simply stays away from them. He knows that they bite! He does not need to prove that again. Consequently, he never learns that most dogs do not bite given ordinary circumstances. In other words, the intense anxiety prevents the student from discovering how unrealistic or overgeneralized his fears actually are. Viewed in this light, it is easy to see why fears are resistant to extinction and why this person fails to develop new modes of adjustment. The implications of these three factors—their ease of information, strong tendency to spread, and durability—for classroom management will be developed in the rest of this section.

DESENSITIZATION PROCEDURES

Basic Factors in Desensitization

The use of desensitization procedures, which constitute one of the most commonly used methods with anxious phobic youngsters, is well illustrated in the classic case of Peter and the rabbit. Peter would, for unknown reasons, become severely anxious when exposed to animals and to a variety of other furry objects such as fur rugs, fur coats, and feathers. Because the rabbit elicited the strongest emotional reaction from Peter, it was selected as the stimulus to be neutralized. This fear was overcome by feeding Peter his favorite food when the rabbit was in the room. Initially the rabbit was caged and placed some distance from Peter. Gradually the caged rabbit was brought closer and closer while Peter was eating until eventually, one day, the rabbit was released from the cage. During the later stages of treatment, Peter did not object if the rabbit was placed on the feeding table or even in his lap. In fact, he spoke fondly of the animal that once terrified him. Peter had become desensitized.

Basically, there are four components that have been singled out as especially relevant to this type of reconditioning process, and they are apparent in the case of Peter and the rabbit.[2] (1) First, it is necessary to identify the event or situation that arouses strong emotion. Peter was upset by many furry objects, but the rabbit was identified as the source of greatest emotional disturbance. (2) One must select a stimulus that is powerful enough to counteract the anxiety associated with the given situation or event. In Peter's case, his favorite food was used as the anxiety-reducing or neutralizing stimulus. In addition to appetizing foods, affection and social reassurance, games, self-assertion techniques, muscular relaxation, positive imagery and tranquilizing drugs also have been used to inhibit or to counteract the anxiety associated with a given situation.

[2] As Bandura (1969) notes, desensitization procedures have much in common with extinction procedures in that they can both weaken avoidant behaviors. The two techniques differ, however, in that (1) desensitization procedures combine fear-arousing and pleasant stimuli whereas in extinction procedures the threatening events are presented alone; (2) there is apt to be considerably less anxiety elicited with desensitization procedures because careful efforts are made to present the threatening situations in attenuated form.

The responsiveness of children to personal warmth and affection helps to neutralize anxiety by offering the child a sense of security and comfort. For example, the presence of a warm teacher can help overcome the anxiety associated with reading in the case of a disabled reader. Likewise, many remedial teachers have made effective use of reading games to overcome a student's fear of reading. In regard to the use of personal reassurance, any significant individual, be he teacher, peer, or principal, can offer personal support and assurance to help desensitize various situations.[3] Likewise assertive behaviors (a polite refusal, a sincere expression of praise, asking a favor, an exclamation of happiness or anger) can serve to inhibit anxiety (Krumboltz and Thoresen, 1969). The examples at the end of the chapter contain illustrations of how peers and teachers have been used effectively in this way. Physical relaxation, positive imagery, and tranquilizing drugs generally have not been used by teachers. (3) Having decided on a powerful anxiety-reducing stimulus to counteract or to nullify the student's intense anxiety, the next step is to expose the anxious student to the frightening situation *in small doses.* In other words, you must provide opportunities to master a threatening situation by dealing with it a little at a time. The student must confront the situation he fears but on a graduated basis. By presenting the fear-arousing situation in attenuated form, the anxiety reactions to be overcome are relatively weak and therefore, can be easily desensitized.

As the weak items lose their anxiety-arousing capacity, the student can be exposed to progressively more threatening stimuli until the individual is eventually able to face the object, event, or situation that he fears most. In the case of Peter, the rabbit was moved closer on a gradual basis and was kept caged until it had eventually lost its anxiety-producing ability.

To insure a gradual approach, it is often helpful to build an anxiety hierarchy in which ten to twenty situations are arranged from those only slightly anxiety-arousing to those that elicit extreme fright. (Several examples of anxiety hierarchies are given later in this chapter). Although such hierarchies are ideally tailor-made to the specific fears of a given child, we might well witness the development of standardized hierarchies for use with anxious students who have similar fears. As Emery and Krumboltz (1967) indicate, "The individualized hierarchies from many subjects with the same problem may be similar enough in content to permit their compilation into a single standard hierarchy." The feasibility of this approach is suggested by research indicating that the use of a standard

---

[3] Psychoanalytically oriented therapists have also made effective use of appetizing foods in counteracting the anxiety of emotionally disturbed children (Bettelheim, 1950).

hierarchy is as effective as individualized hierarchies in reducing test anxiety among college freshman. In addition to the area of test anxiety, standard hierarchies probably could also be constructed for anxieties that are associated with entrance into first grade or high school, reading, job interviews, and the like. Group desensitization also might be feasible for students with common anxieties.

Desensitization hierarchies can be set-up along various dimensions (Bandura, 1969). They can be ordered in terms of physical proximity to the feared situation. For example, one step in the hierarchy for a school-phobic youngster might consist in going to the bus stop in the morning. Temporal dimensions have also been used in establishing anxiety hierarchies by varying the time proximity to the feared event. For instance, helping the student to relax while studying the night before the exam could constitute one step in a temporally graduated hierarchy that is designed to overcome test anxiety. Next, one might help the test-anxious student to relax the morning of the exam. One can also vary the symbolic-reality dimension in ordering items on a hierarchy. The teacher, for instance, could have a student imagine or even role play a feared situation if the anxious student were too threatened by the real life objects or situations. Or the teacher might have him read about someone with a similar fear and determine how he overcame it. Later, as approximations of the frightening event lose much of their emotional reactivity for the student, he might want actually to experience the once threatening situation. (4) Finally, one must temporally pair the anxiety-reducing stimulus, for example, one's favorite food with the frightening situation, for example, the rabbit. By repeatedly associating the unpleasant situation with something pleasant, the threatening situation gradually loses its ability to generate anxiety in the student, and the child begins to develop more positive reactions to the object that he previously feared.

Cautions and Guidelines

As with other techniques, there are certain limitations or cautions of which the teacher should be aware. Sometimes the rewards associated with avoidant behavior are greater than the ones associated with overcoming the fear. The school-phobic youngster, for instance, might find staying at home and the fuss made over him more rewarding than conquering his fear of school. In such instances, it is necessary to remove the rewards maintaining the avoidant behavior and to increase the rewards associated with restored functioning. Second, there is a real danger that the steps in the anxiety hierarchy are not small enough. That is, we might be trying to expose the anxious student to threatening situations before he is ready for them. Be sure that there is a number of small steps so that the individual is not overwhelmed with anxiety when he is exposed to them. A third problem arises when the phobic youngster's anxieties have a realistic basis. In cases of this nature, desensitization alone will not prove adequate in modifying the fear. Other techniques might profitably be combined with desensitization procedures when the anxiety is a realistic consequence of behavioral deficits. A boy who is a "sissy" and afraid of aggressive games might, for example, need to be taught more masculine ways of behavior via positive reward and modeling. Similarly, a disabled reader who fears the printed page will have to be assisted in promoting his reading skills before he can be fully desensitized. Finally, it is not always an easy matter to identify the critical sources of anxiety. Consider the case of the anxious reader. Should we desensitize his fear of reading? Or should we focus on his fear of parental rejection, his intense sibling rivalry, or a fear of leaving his mother at home? The problem is complicated in that an individual's anxieties may be under multiple stimulus control (Bandura, 1969). When in doubt as to the source of the anxiety, the teacher would do well to consult with the school psychologist or counselor.

ADDITIONAL MANAGEMENT CONSIDERATIONS

In addition to desensitization techniques, there are certain other strategies that the teacher should bear in mind when attempting to further the anxious-withdrawn child's personal and academic adjustment.

1. Recognize that teacher praise is often not a reward for the shy child, at least, not initially. These youngsters commonly have unfavorable self-concepts, and the praise given by the teacher is at odds with what others have communicated to them and with what they believe about themselves. Consequently, the teacher's use of praise generates dissonance and makes the child feel uncomfortable. In instances where verbal approval produces unfavorable classroom behaviors, such as discomfort, defensiveness, unrealistic aspirations, and incredibility (they suspect such nice words), the teacher might well consider the use of tangible or activity rewards. For instance, one elementary school student with a low self-estimate but high standards would typically tear up and discard art or written assignments whenever the teacher praised her in front of the class. This student, however, could accept points to be spent on activity rewards selected from a reinforcement menu and nonverbal praise in the form of written comments on her assignments ("Not bad! That was a tough

assignment")(In brief, although there are aspects of teacher praise that the shy withdrawn child may like, be alert to the possibility that praise may sometimes assume partly aversive qualities. This type of ambivalent reaction should not deter the use of rewards, however. In fact, don't let this child turn you off, that is, extinguish your rewarding behavior. (Shy, withdrawn children are adept at getting others to leave them alone.) Accept the fact that the finding of rewards will be a ticklish job and consider the initial use of other kinds of rewards to modify behavior. Recognize that the anxious-withdrawn child needs and responds well to teacher warmth in order to feel safe and secure, but that this warmth may be best conveyed to the student in a nonverbal fashion.

2. Consider the use of the peer group in drawing out the shy child. Direct attention from an omniscient and omnipotent teacher often makes the anxious withdrawn child feel more self-conscious and insecure with the result that withdrawal tendencies become even more pronounced. Select a student with whom the shy child feels somewhat comfortable and have him assist the retiring individual in becoming more outgoing and assertive. For example, the teacher might say something like, "Jim, I think Jerry (the withdrawn child) might like to play this game with you. Why don't you ask him."

3. Programmed instruction also seems to hold considerable promise as an instructional device for the anxious withdrawn student. Whereas anxiety typically interferes with the learning of complex intellectual tasks like those required in school, it tends to facilitate the learning of simple conditioned responses. Our task then becomes one of making appropriate academic responses simple, and programmed instruction is one approach to accomplishing just this (Quay, 1963). By breaking down complex tasks into simpler sequences (and thereby approximating a conditioning model), we have transformed what was once a deterent force into a facilitating one. What was once the student's disability has now become a source of strength. Programmed instruction also minimizes anxiety by insuring a high rate of success or correct answers. This helps him to develop greater self-assurance and, thereby, increases the probability of a more assertive approach to life.

4. Give the anxious student opportunities to overlearn the skill(s) so as to bolster his confidence. We can all remember how helpful it was to prepare for anxiety-producing events (our first date,

our first exam in college, our first job interview). Preparation can take forms such as self-rehearsal, role playing, or watching others as you will learn in the examples at the end of the chapter.

5. Anxious students respond well to structure, which refers to the setting up of a definite, dependable, and consistent classroom routine. This student needs a predictable classroom environment. Many aggressive, acting-out students are novelty seekers and thrive on frequent change in daily routines, but this is not the case with anxious-withdrawn individuals. Novelty for them is threatening, since in learning new concepts or in adjusting to new situations, they are not sure what is going to happen next, and this is upsetting. Available research indicates that highly anxious students learn better in structured classroom settings than they do in unstructured ones. Teachers should be alert to the fact that these students require extra attention when new concepts or skills are being introduced, since this involves change, which means that uncertainty and anxiety will intensify and, perhaps, interfere with the assimilation of these new ideas. For example, even shifting from division by one digit to division by two digits may prove anxiety producing to these students. A little extra instructional attention and personal support at these transition points will prove well worth the time invested by the teacher. Gradually, the anxious student can be exposed to less structured tasks.

6. When disciplinary action is required, do not rush in and over-whelm them. Anxious, withdrawn students are usually very much aware of what the ground rules are, and they do not need the reality rub-in that many aggressive students need. Furthermore, the shy student is typically very sensitive to negative appraisal and evaluation by others. Thus, it is not ordinarily necessary for the teacher to be severe with these pupils. Mere eye contact may be all that is needed to remedy the situation. Or you may simply say something to the effect that you know that he is generally well intentioned even though he did slip on this occasion. There is no need to use an elephant gun to kill a field mouse.

EXAMPLES OF DESENSITIZATION PROCEDURES

Problem: Fear of speaking in a group

Technique: Desensitization plus positive reward

Mickey was a bright sixth grade girl who was referred to the school counselor because she became acutely anxious when asked to read, to give a report, or to perform in any way before her peers. Although she would participate in class discussions and had warm relationships with others, she had always been unable to speak before a group despite her desire to be able to do so. A conference was held, and it was explained that "learning a behavior a little at a time in a relaxed manner" can often help people perform behaviors that previously caused appreciable anxiety. Mickey met with her school counselor once a week for six weeks. During these sessions, she role-played behaviors involved in giving an oral report. Initially, she role-played getting out of her seat and coming to the front of the room. Practice in oral reading was also undertaken but this was done initially when Mickey was still in her seat. The variety and length of activities were increased weekly. Liberal reinforcement was given for gains made, for example, "Hey, that's great!" and progress was constantly called to her attention. She was encouraged to rehearse these behaviors but only if she felt comfortable in doing so.

A plan of action was designed to gradually increase her oral participation in front of her classmates. Mickey was included in a social studies committee that gave weekly reports on various countries which they were studying. She did not have to participate beyond a point that made her anxious, however. Her first role consisted in standing by a large map at the front of the classroom and pointing out regions which were being discussed by other members of the committee. Later, members of the committee, at the prompting of the teachers, increased Mickey's role by asking questions that on intellectual grounds alone, she could readily handle, for example, "What's the region called north of Paris?" Mickey was thanked by other members for her active role, and she was told that she had done a fine job. The seating arrangement of the committee, while giving the report, was that of a semicircle and Mickey's seat was situated so that she did not have to directly face the audience. Mickey gradually became more relaxed while giving reports in front of the class. By the end of the school year, Mickey had reached the point that she volunteered to give an oral report on class accomplishments in social studies (Hosford, 1969).

Note. This case illustrates the combined use of gradual exposure to threatening situations, the pairing of unpleasant tasks (talking in front of the class) with something pleasant (peer and teacher approval served as the anxiety-neutralizing stimulus), and the use of role playing or rehearsal (overlearning). School personnel were careful not to overwhelm the student by forcing her into situations in which the anxiety was unbearable; yet, they also were careful to give her opportunities to confront the feared situation. Intrinsic rewards were also probably operative in that she was happy to master her difficulty.

. . .

Problem: Nonparticipation in gym activities

Technique: A combination of desensitization, modeling, and positive reward

Jim was an eleven-year-old boy who transferred from another school district. His passivity and lack of assertiveness pervaded all aspects of his classroom adjustment but were most noticeable in gym class. He seemed interested in but afraid of athletic activities, as evidenced by his hovering on the fringe of the action. The teacher's attempts to involve him directly were met with stubborn resistance by Jim. A gradual approach seemed indicated, and the following sequence of steps was tentatively established.

1. Reading exciting stories about baseball players.
2. Going onto the playground.
3. Observing his peers play softball.
4. Occasionally retrieving a stray ball.
5. Keeping score.
6. Listening to the athletically oriented conversation of his peers.
7. Having peers relate some of the "fun times" they had in gym class.
8. Having peers tell how much they liked the gym teacher and how he helped them learn new games and skills.
9. Asking Jim's best friend to "help him get used to the gym program" at this school.
10. Walking to gym class with a friend after school to inspect the gym and athletic equipment.
11. Having Jim's friend introduce him to the gym teacher while visiting the gym after school.
12. Gym teacher offers to let the boys use some of the equipment for a short while after school.
13. Going to gym class with his friend during the regularly scheduled time.
14. Changing into gym clothes.
15. Keeping score.
16. Starting with activities that are in keeping with Jim's interests and abilities, for example, running.
17. Allowing him to practice certain skills with his friend, for example, shooting free throws.
18. Putting him into games but assigning him a position or role that does not overwhelm him.

19. Gradually exposing him to athletic activities that involve greater physical contact.
20. Giving him occasional leadership roles.

Comment. Notice that the beginning steps involved a very minimum of anxiety in that they took place outside of the gym area and did not force actual participation. Once Jim enjoyed the earlier phases of the program (steps 1 to 8), he was given gradual exposure to the gym area itself. Finally, athletic activities themselves were introduced. A number of strategies were used in facilitating Jim's adjustment to the physical education program. Foremost among them were the gradual exposure to anxiety-producing situations, the use of peer models, guided participation (his friend's help as an anxiety-reducing strategy), and the use of feedback and peer rewards.

• • •

Problem: Fear of doing art projects
Technique: Desensitization and modeling

Many kindergarten and primary level students are inhibited with regard to art activities. Frequently, they will not participate or put forth only a halfhearted effort. Since this problem is not uncommon, one teacher finally decided to develop the following set of procedures to cope with it.

1. Watch parent cutting, pasting, or painting at home.
2. Work on different art projects with family members and/or mother alone.
3. In school, have the class discuss some art projects that they want to do throughout the year.
4. The teacher has certain students tell how much fun they have had in doing similar art projects.
5. Ask a child to contribute to discussions on what students like to do at home.
6. Observe art projects at school exhibits (other classes' works) or visit a gallery in town.
7. During art period, listen to the explanations of art projects to be done.
8. Watch a demonstration of media by the teacher.
9. Be a monitor or distributor of materials to the other children.
10. Observe other children working on projects.
11. Work as member of a group of children on an art project, for ex-

ample, class mural or mobile (but give him a small role to perform).

12. As one member of a group, have him first distribute materials, then paint or fill in lines drawn by other children, and finally have a small section or part for which he is responsible to complete.

13. Work with another person (best friend) on an art project with the child taking more responsibility each time toward the completion of the project.

14. Have him start alone on an easy art project (for example, one in which he would be responsible in chosing colors of outlines by teacher).

15. Complete easy projects.

Comment. Note how the student was gradually introduced to the art activities. At first the student could watch others have fun in their artwork (and hopefully model their behavior). As students became familiarized with the feared situation, they could be given greater exposure to the threatening art activities. Also, bear in mind that the use of others (parents, teachers, and peers) to guide the phobic student through the anxiety hierarchy is one of the best ways of overcoming fears.

• • •

Problem: Fear of reading

Technique: Densensitization hierarchy

Chuck is a primary student who avoids reading because of early failure experience. He started school before he was intellectually and emotionally ready with the result that he failed to make satisfactory progress in reading. Realizing that Chuck had to overcome the anxiety associated with reading, the teacher devised the following anxiety hierarchy.

1. Sits down with a small reading group.
2. Listens during presentation of vocabulary chart or drill.
3. Participates with the group as they practice rhymes or refrains during group story.
4. Reads off words that he contributed from a reading chart.
5. Dictates short sentences which teacher writes on his chart.
6. Practices reading these sentences to teacher and/or classmates.
7. Dictates one paragraph at a time about things he observed or was interested in.

8. Reads these paragraphs to the teacher, classmates, or into tape recorder.
9. Dictates longer stories to teacher.
10. Practices these stories, illustrating them and compiling them onto his own book.
11. Reads comic strips and easy interesting materials (rhymes, jokes) that teacher gathers on his reading level.
12. Reads a sentence (or paragraph) from a book at his reading level and in his interest level.
13. Reading is lengthened in the above-mentioned book.
14. Place him in a reading group.
15. Presentation of story in the assigned reading text (being sure that he is able to read the words).
16. Lengthen reading sessions as warranted—first a sentence, then a paragraph, then a page, and so on.

Comment. In addition to providing small doses at a time, the teacher used her own presence and personal reassurance to minimize the student's anxiety. Notice that guided participation by the teacher is an especially effective means of helping the student work through the anxiety hierarchy.

•   •   •

Problem: Fear of asserting self in intellectual pursuits
Technique: Desensitization, modeling, positive reward, and extinction

In every classroom there are passive students who let (in fact, almost invite) other students to take advantage of them. This problem of passivity and withdrawal readily manifests itself in competitive academic pursuits. In an attempt to make such students more assertive, three teachers collaborated in devising the following list.

1. After having read a story to the class about a boy who stood up for his rights or point of view, have class discussion about the value of asserting oneself when the situation calls for it.
2. Reward classmates when they take the initiative in relation to others, when they sell their ideas, and when they defend their rights or viewpoints. Ignore individuals who withdraw from situations or who accept being imposed upon.
3. Sit child next to someone who asserts himself and solicit this

students' help in making the passive child more assertive. Caution your helper about the need for taking small steps.

4. Have role-playing situations where one child readily gives in and the passive student asserts himself.

5. Play educationally oriented games that call for the defending of acquired "property" (for example, amount of vocabulary cards, amount of play money accumulated).

6. Praise child when he is able to "stand his ground" in the game situation.

7. In class discussions, call on child to participate in a subject in which he feels confident (for example, some concept or topic in which you have worked individually with him).

8. Have student present a controversial viewpoint in an area of interest to him and have him give his conclusions.

9. Encourage other students to question him about a controversial subject in which he is knowledgeable and have a prestigeful peer support his view.

These teachers found that many of their intellectually passive students became more forward under the above regimen; the students verbalized feelings of pride over their new boldness, and classroom discussion flourished to a greater extent.

Comment. This case illustrates how other techniques can be effectively combined with desensitization procedures.

. . .

Problem: School phobia

Technique: Desensitization procedures, positive reward, and educational (contingency) contracting

A contingency contract was arranged in which the following steps were used in treating the case of a school phobic girl (Cantrell et al., 1969).

    Getting out of bed—5 points
    Getting dressed—5 points
    Eating breakfast—5 points
    No crying before school—5 points
    No illness before school—5 points
    Getting on school bus—5 points
    Approaching the class—5 points

Going into classroom—5 points
Staying in class—5 points per 15 minutes
No sickness at school—5 points
No crying at school—5 points
Homework started with no reminders—15 points
Homework started with one reminder—10 points
Homework started with two reminders—5 points
Homework completed—5 points

The points earned could be exchanged for various activities outside of school as follows.

Activity	Cost
Watching TV	25 points per 30 minutes
Renting toys or books	25 points per 30 minutes
Helping mother in the kitchen	25 points per 30 minutes
Outdoor play	50 points per 30 minutes
Having friends over	100 points per 30 minutes
Visiting at the home of a friend	100 points per 30 minutes
Going out privilege	150 points per 30 minutes
Overnight visit	200 points per 30 minutes
Spending money	1 point per penny

This girl was also offered a bonus of one new article of clothing for going to school one full week. Full attendance at school without resistance was obtained a week and one half after the contract was initiated. Moreover, she remained in school for the rest of that and the next school year.

Comment. This study illustrates the practice of taking small steps and of making the receiving of rewards contingent on the completion of steps toward the desired behavior that has been spelled out in a behavioral contract. Although the rewards in this instance were administered outside of the school situation, most teachers or counselors would probably also take advantage of rewards inherent in the school setting, especially since the parents of school phobics often have trouble being firm in their disciplinary practices.

·   ·   ·

Problem: Fear of job interviews
Technique: Desensitization hierarchy

Many students, especially anxious ones, are afraid of being critically evaluated by authority figures. One form of evaluation occurs during job interviews. What follows is an anxiety hierarchy that was developed for a particular high school senior who was apprehensive about job interviews.

1. Secure occupational information from teachers, friends, and the school counselor.
2. Decide on the kinds of jobs wanted.
3. Complete a list of your qualifications for the various jobs including educational backgrounds complete with names, dates, and addresses of schools attended, work experiences with names of supervisors, dates, rate of pay, and how these prior experiences might help you in performing this job, and several references with phone numbers and addresses.
4. Decide what you will say on meeting your prospective employer.
5. Practice filling out a variety of application blanks.
6. Anticipate questions that you might be asked, for example, "Will you be going back to school in the fall?"
7. Think about the kinds of questions you might ask so as to make a favorable impression.
8. Role-play the job interview with a friend, a teacher, or a parent, and try to discover ways to improve your interview.
9. Decide what you might say on termination of the interview.
10. Phone the number listed in the classified section for an appointment to interview.
11. Check the location of and the best route to the interview location.
12. Make a practice drive to interview location, checking travel time, parking facilities, building entrances, and location of personnel office.
13. Decide what kind of clothes would be most appropriate.
14. Go to personnel office a little early.
15. Fill out application blank while waiting to see interviewer.
16. Meet with interviewer.
17. Follow up on interview if necessary.

Comment. Fear of job interviews might well constitute one area in which a reasonable degree of standardization of anxiety hierarchies is possible.

•   •   •

Problem: Test anxiety

Technique: Vicarious desensitization, modeling

One high school youth was referred to the school counselor in an effort to reduce the anxiety associated with math examinations. The counselor decided that he would have the student view photographs of another student going through the steps of the following test anxiety hierarchy.

1. Signing up for a math class.
2. Going to first class, hearing assignments, and finding out when the exams will be given.
3. Getting notes for a class he missed.
4. Engaging in a weekly review session.
5. Discussing the exam with a bright achievement-oriented student who says that it will be a tough test.
6. Reviewing old exams and seeing how much you know.
7. Studying the evening before the exam.
8. Seeing how late it is and how much material you still have to study.
9. Conducting a last-minute review to cram in the things you don't know as well as you would like to.
10. Coming into the room on exam day.
11. Getting the exam and writing your name on it.
12. Skimming the exam and running across items the answers to which are not immediately evident.
13. Instructor interrupts your train of thought to correct errors in typing.
14. Teacher throws out an ambiguous item that you were sure you knew the answer to.
15. Finding yourself stuck on a question and seeing everyone else busy working.
16. Noticing your bright achievement-oriented friend hand in his paper 30 minutes after the exam began.
17. Realizing that only 5 minutes remain on the exam and that you still have several items left to do.
18. Talking to fellow students after the exam and finding out that they answered the questions differently.
19. Coming into class the next day to get your grade on the exam.

In each counseling session, this adolescent boy was asked to imagine items selected from the anxiety hierarchy. Following twenty such sessions, which were spread out over the course of a semester, the student was able to imagine the most threatening item on the list. (The anxious student often experiences his greatest difficulty in the face of personal evaluation, for example, receiving a grade on an exam).

Comment. Note that anxiety-producing events need not always be presented in real life form. In certain instances, it may be too difficult to recreate life conditions and/or too anxiety-provoking to do so. Under either circumstance, the frightening situation might be presented pictorially, in story form, or through the use of miniature objects.

In the above case, the personal support of the counselor was used as a pleasant stimulus to neutralize the student's anxiety. Overcoming his fear was also probably quite intrinsically rewarding. The success achieved in this case also can be attributed to the fact that this student was not deficient in terms of the academic skills needed for mastery of the subject matter. The possibilities for a standard anxiety hierarchy are also apparent.

SUMMARY

A moderate amount of anxiety is desirable in that it foster's the student's academic and social well-being. High anxiety, however, can be a crippling force that has rather wide ranging adverse effects on the student's personality and intellectual adjustment. Also being unsuccessful in one's efforts "to reach" an anxious withdrawn student does much to undermine a teacher's sense of competence. It is not surprising, therefore, that teachers are generally baffled and bewildered by these students. Pressured by the demands of 30 other students and unrewarded for their efforts to "draw-out" the shy student, teachers are prone to let the withdrawn student be. Thus, in a very genuine sense, the teacher unintentionally reinforces the shy student's withdrawal tendencies. Instead of allowing the shy student to escape from threatening situations, the teacher should provide opportunities for the student to confront them by taking a small step at a time. In implementing desensitization procedures, care should be given to the selection of an anxiety-reducing stimulus that can be paired with the frightening situation. It is also essential that the anxious student be exposed to the frightening situation in attenuated form which is only gradually increased to its highest level. The possibilities of standard anxiety hierarchies and group desensitization procedures, although largely unexplored at present, seem to hold considerable promise. The use of multiple procedures, for example, combining positive reward, modeling and desensitization techniques, can be a very powerful means of altering maladaptive avoidant behaviors. Other techniques that have proved of value in facilitating the anxious student's adjustment to school include the use of structure, programmed instruction, overlearning, and mild forms of discipline.

REFERENCES

Bandura, A. *Principles of Behavior Modification*. New York: Holt, Rinehart and Winston, Inc., 1969.

Bettelheim, B. *Love is Not Enough*. New York: Collier Books, 1950.

Cantrell, R., Cantrell, M., Huddleston, C., and Woolridge, R. Contingency contracting with school problems. *Journal of Applied Behavior Analysis*, 1969, 2, 215–220.

Emery, J., and Krumboltz, J. Standard versus individualized hierarchies in desensitization to reduce test anxiety. *Journal of Counseling Psychology*, 1967, 14, 204–209.

Krumboltz, J., and Thoresen, C. *Behavioral Counseling*. New York: Holt, Rinehart and Winston, Inc., 1969.

Morse, W., and Wingo, G. *Psychology and Teaching*, Third Edition, New York: Scott Foresman, 1969.

Quay, H. Some basic considerations in the education of emotionally disturbed children. Except. Child., 1963, 30, 27–31.

Ruebush, B. Anxiety in H. W. Stevenson (ed.), *Child Psychology, The Sixty-Second Yearbook of the National Society for the Study of Education, Part 1*. Chicago: The University of Chicago Press, 1963, pp. 460–516.

7

Implementing Positive Disciplinary Procedures

Thus far we have focused on the five principles or strategies that can facilitate the academic and personal adjustment of students and at the same time reduce wear-and-tear on the teacher. But it is one thing to have knowledge of these techniques and quite another thing to translate this knowledge into daily classroom practice. Unless we can implement this knowledge, all is for naught as far as actual practice is concerned. The reader might, naturally enough, think that these techniques would be readily incorporated into management tactics because of their demonstrated effectives. Unfortunately life, as any practitioner will tell you, is not that easy. In this chapter we discuss the necessity for a careful consideration of this critical process of implementation, some of the problems typically associated with it, and some ways to go about it. Our discussion, following the lead of Woody (1969), will center around four areas that demand consideration.

EDUCATIONAL PHILOSOPHY

It is not uncommon for teachers to be exposed to an educational philosophy that exerts contradictory demands on teachers. For instance, it is widely believed in certain circles that self-control develops best in an atmosphere of self-responsibility. There is certainly a fair degree of validity in this belief. The difficulty arises, however, when the student left to his self-direction, behaves in ways that are not viewed by others as adaptive or wholesome. The public reaction is one of indignation, and the teachers are roundly criticized for allowing students to run wild. "There is the demand that educators must not be human cyberneticians, manipulative programers of human behavior; yet they must also be responsible for assuring that the students will display acceptable behavior at all times (Woody, 1969)." All teachers are exposed to these philosophical contradictions and must learn to cope with them.

Despite the scientific basis for the techniques discussed in this text, it would be naive to expect that they will match the educational philosophies under which many teachers must operate. The teachers who use rewards as a means of modifying behavior might be charged with using bribery. The teacher who uses aversive controls might be branded as hostile. Or the teacher who uses these principles systematically might be accused of treating children like robots or Pavlov's dog. The teacher as well as other psychoeducational staff who use these techniques must thoroughly expect and prepare to deal with such conflicts, resistances, and expressions of skepticism. The handling of these problems ordinarily involves debate, discussion, critical analysis, and compromise.

INVOLVEMENT OF COLLEAGUES

Because students frequently have more than one caretaker in the school setting, it is essential to have intrastaff and interdisciplinary cooperation if the maximum benefit from these techniques is to be obtained. Woody (1969) contends that individuals who object to behavior modification techniques do so on one of two grounds. There are those who resist because they do not understand or appreciate the procedures on rational grounds. And there are those who are unwilling to accept these principles because of personality factors in their own makeup. The immediate observable and durable changes in the behavior of problem students is, perhaps, the best weapon in overcoming such resistances. Admittedly, however, it is unrealistic to expect total support for any system of disciplinary practices.

It is important that school administrators be given special attention during the orientation process (Woody, 1969). For, while they have little direct contact with students, they are in large measure responsible for casting the basic philosophy of disciplinary strategies. Although detailed expositions are unnecessary, the potency of these techniques should certainly be made clear to administrators by the school psychologist or counselor.

The teacher is a key person in the success of any disciplinary program. As noted at the outset of this work, our basic premise is that the teacher can modify the behavior of his students. Again, resistances can be expected. Foremost among the several factors that seem to underlie teacher resistance to consultative help on classroom discipline are the omniscient attitudes of many consultants, the dearth of practical advice given by consultants, the controversial aspects of behavior modification principles (for example, punishment), and the personal threat to the teacher's sense of competence. For whatever combination of reasons, it is not uncommon to find that teachers often behave toward the consultant much like an oppositional student behaves toward them. If we are to recruit the assistance of teachers, we will need to use vehicles such as coffee-cup seminars and in-service training programs (especially for the beginning teacher) which offer opportunity for frank discussions, role playing, audiovisual aids depicting the use of behavior modification principles, "how-to-do-it yourself" books on discipline, and tips on how to implement these principles in the classroom. The following guidelines should prove helpful to school mental health specialists in developing meaningful in-service training sessions.

1. Secure administrative support for the in-service program so that the teachers will know that the techniques to be discussed have official backing.

2. Attendance should be on a voluntary basis or, perhaps, mandatory for first-year teachers.

3. Encourage teachers to discuss the kinds of disciplinary problems they are experiencing. All teachers experience some difficulty in handling problem students, but many are reluctant to talk about these instances with their colleagues.

4. Use lectures spiced with earthy examples to illustrate the techniques of behavior change. Films and readings of a practical nature on classroom management also should be suggested.

5. Help the group to set up specific target behaviors that are observable and thus countable.

6. Provide practice in planning ways to strengthen appropriate behaviors and to weaken undesired behaviors.

7. Use actual cases that the teachers have encountered. It is sometimes a good idea to deal with the most difficult cases so as to demonstrate the effectiveness of behavior modification techniques.

8. Let the teachers know that you are available to meet with them regarding problem students. You may want to schedule conferences at regular intervals.

9. In difficult cases, the actual observation of the child in the classroom is suggested. If this is not possible, perhaps the teacher could use a tape recorder to provide a realistic and detailed account of what the problem student does.

10. Seek suggestions from other teachers in the group. Every school has teachers whose talent for practical ingenuity is truly amazing.

11. Be sure to reward the teacher for using these techniques in their classrooms. Consistent reinforcement is particularly desirable when teachers are first putting these principles into practice. The building principal, school counselor, and fellow teachers can play an important role here if alerted to the significance of it.

12. In very difficult cases, it may be necessary for the consultant to go into the classroom and actually model appropriate ways of handling unacceptable behavior. These demonstrations might then be followed by observation of the teacher's attempts to imitate and practice these techniques. Role-playing can also be a useful in-service method.

13. Use a school newsletter describing the actual handling of problem students as a teaching and advertising technique.

ORIENTING THE LAY COMMUNITY

The primary purpose of orienting the lay community is to gain acceptance and support for the use of the school's disciplinary policy and strategies. The orientation is not designed to explain the specifics of these principles. "Rather the emphasis is on familiarizing them with the reasons why behavior should be modified, what behavior should be modified, why the school and its professional personnel hold this responsibility, and how they, the community, can facilitate this process" (Woody, 1969).

There is another value that occurs from community orientation, namely, the recruitment of active lay involvement. There is a growing body of knowledge showing that nonprofessionals can learn and effectively apply these techniques. Although not yet widely accepted among professional educators, nonprofessionals cast in the role of teacher aids could play a very important part in promoting and maintaining classroom control. That we have not tapped the valuable resources of nonprofessionals available in every community is, indeed, regrettable.

In conclusion, remember that orientation efforts never end.

PROFESSIONAL TRAINING

At present, there are few teacher training programs that offer adequate training in behavior modification. The implications for training are two-fold. For those already in the field, it will be necessary to rely on in-service training sessions, institutes, and workshops. School mental health specialists (counselors, psychologists, social workers) will hopefully honor their obligations in regard to consulting with teachers on matters of classroom management. The assumption of a consultative role of this type demands a redefinition of job role for many of these specialists. Psychologists will have to do less diagnostic testing, school social workers will have to dispense with some of their play therapy sessions with children, and school counselors will have to come out from under their paperwork. Role redefinition is never easy. Professionals like others, prefer not to give up security-producing modes of operation (even if these models of intervention fail to meet the needs of teachers and students) for unfamiliar, untried roles in which they are not fully prepared. Although some school mental health specialists will undoubtedly not want to train teachers and nonprofessional aides in the use of behavior modification principles, there are increasing signs of such readiness in many school districts. Hopefully, the "hard-core" professional specialists will prove more adaptable than the "hard-core" students with whom they must deal. One interesting approach entails the use of a school newsletter that illustrates the use and value of behavior modification principles through use of the case study (SALT). Other counselors and psychologists have wisely relied on the experience and practical ingenuity of seasoned teachers in their in-service sessions and workshops. In addition to in-service education, it is imperative that the psychoeducational specialists visit classrooms and reinforce teachers for their use of these techniques. In the more difficult cases, the consultant might visit the classroom and actually demonstrate the use of these techniques. As Krumboltz and Thoresen (1969) note, "Skilled leadership is required to help some teachers try a new approach. Sometimes a useful approach consists of 'How about trying it for a week to see what happens?'"

There must also be change in teacher training programs at the university level. This may pose a number of curriculum and personnel problems. Woody (1969) points out that training should ideally be given at the undergraduate level in learning theory, childhood psychopathology, personality theory, and guidance and counseling. Perhaps even more important is the need for supervised experience in the use of these behavior change techniques. Hopefully, as the teacher shortage disappears, colleges of education will be able to focus more on the quality aspects

of training and will devote increased attention to the development of
effective skills in discipline.

ETHICAL CONSIDERATIONS

Thus far, we have addressed ourselves to the question of *how* we can
change unacceptable behavior. That is, emphasis has been devoted to
techniques for modifying behavior. As our knowledge in this area increases, another question immediately demands increased attention,
namely, *what* behaviors should we try to change. Stated differently, what
constitutes acceptable and unacceptable classroom behavior? Should we
insist on silence at all times or should orderly communication be our objective? Should John be allowed to pick his nose or is it the teacher's
business or right to stop him? Should students be allowed to wear long
hair or should they be expelled if they do so? Should we impose our
values on the lower class student or should we accept his behavior as it
is? Should we try to make all quiet students more gregarious or should
we permit them to follow their own life style? Basically, these questions
center around the issues of values and freedom of choice. There are, of
course, no easy answers to these complex questions but the following
general guidelines should prove helpful in deciding what behaviors
should be changed.

1. If a behavior interferes with a student's own performance or with
the class's performance, then consideration might well be given to
modifying it.

2. On the other hand, student behaviors that the teacher finds personally annoying (for example, leg swinging while seated) but that
are not disruptive to the individual student or the group might well
be permitted by the teacher. In these instances, it is necessary for
the teacher to examine his own personal and cultural values in an
effort to become more tolerant of individual differences.

3. It is often helpful to distinguish between two kinds of rules—
those established for purposes of managerial efficiency and those designed to promote the welfare of the student (Redl and Wineman,
1952). Whenever we deal with large numbers of individuals, many
rules, regulations, and routines are introduced to promote managerial smoothness. For example, in most schools, it is not feasible to
serve all students lunch at the same time. Hence, there is an establishment of lunch shifts. Rules and routines can be evaluated by
another criterion, however, namely, the extent to which they facilitate the growth and development of students. It is easy to see how

the purpose of administrative efficiency can be achieved at the expense of the very purpose for which the institution was formed. Even worse perhaps, is the fact that many rules are arbitrary and fail to serve either of these two purposes. In brief, educators might well reflect on the rules that they have devised to insure that school regulations are consonant with the objective of facilitating the development of students. When implemented in this manner, rules are not disruptive to student morale nor are they a source of unwarranted frustration and resentment.

4. Students should be permitted as much self-direction as they are capable of handling. This generally means a greater sharing of authority as the students advance in development (classroom government, mutually agreed on educational contracts, and the like).[1] Although initially it is frequently necessary to provide adequate external controls, especially with disturbed youth, there should be less need for these controls as the student acquires self-control. Mature self-direction does not arise without opportunities to develop it. Thus the teacher's role at times may consist in informing the student as to possible outcomes of a given behavior, and then in assuming the role of an interested bystander who allows students to experience the natural consequences (favorable as well as unfavorable) of his actions.

REFERENCES

Krumboltz, J., and Thoresen, C. *Behavioral Counseling.* New York: Holt, Rinehart and Winston, Inc., 1969.
Redl, F., and Wineman, D. *Controls From Within.* Glencoe, Illinois: Free Press, 1952.
Woddy, R. *Behavioral Problem Children in the Schools.* New York: Appleton-Century-Crofts, 1969.

[1] To those who would object to any use of external control, it would be well to note that ironically such provisions can eventually enable the individual to achieve greater self-control. In this sense, external controls promote greater individual self-determination by freeing him from his present binding, maladaptive modes of adjustment. Anyone who has worked with disturbed students realizes that (1) they are not "free" to begin with; (2) that they become free from their own irrational impulses as they achieve some degree of self-control; and that (3) there must be external controls provided so internalized self-direction can be fostered. In brief, by expanding the range of one's learned behaviors to include more effective ways of coping, we also expand the individual's freedom to choose in adapting to his surroundings. Learning these new behaviors is, in effect, liberating.

Index